The Earth and the Stars

BY RICHARD WHITTINGHAM AND BARBARA BROOKS

Illustrated by George Suyeoka

Numbers and Discoveries

BY ARTHUR J. SNIDER

Illustrated by James Teason

Fact Book

Illustrated by John Faulkner

The Southwestern Company

Nashville, Tennessee

CONTENTS

The Earth and the Stars

Numbers and Discoveries

1

Fact Book

The Earth
and the Stars

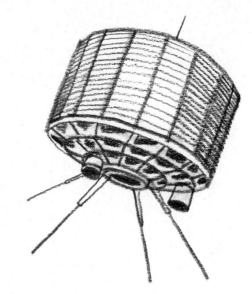

The Earth and the Sky

DAVID STOOD ON the sidewalk and looked up at the sky. It was a clear night. The sky seemed filled with thousands of blinking stars. He also saw a bright, full moon, which seemed much larger than any of the stars.

David heard footsteps on the sidewalk. He turned quickly. It was his father.

"You've been out here a long time," his father said. "What are you looking at?"

"Just the stars," David said. "There sure are a lot of them."

"How about that light over there?" his father asked.

"That's not a star or a planet. That's a satellite," David answered.

"Right! It orbits around the earth just as the moon does," his father said.

"We have a lot of satellites up there," David said.

"And tonight, there really is a man on the moon," his father said. "Not like the old story of the man *in* the moon. We used to say that because the moon sometimes looked like a face. But today a man from earth actually landed on the moon."

David and his father both stared at the round full moon. They wondered what exciting things the astronaut might be doing up there.

At the same time as David and his father were looking at the moon, the astronaut was looking back at the earth. He could see the outlines of continents and oceans. The earth looked very big and beautiful.

The astronaut wished that everyone on earth could see what their world looked like from the moon. Then they would know what a beautiful place it was. They would appreciate the mountains and the valleys, the islands, the oceans, the lakes and the rivers. The astronaut thought about how much there is to learn just about things on earth. And there is even more to learn about outer space. Then he went back to his work. And, on earth, David and his father walked back into their house.

Earth–Our Planet

FROM FAR OUT IN SPACE, the earth looks like a blue-green ball. The miles and miles of blue-green ocean make the land part seem small. Actually, the land on which we live and build cities *is* very small. About three-fourths of the earth is covered by water. Land takes up only one quarter of the earth.

Earth is one of the nine planets in our solar system. It would take 320 planets the size of Earth to make one Jupiter, the largest planet. And it would take 18 planets the size of Mercury, the smallest planet, to make one Earth. Compared to the other planets, Earth is medium in size.

To a man in space, Earth's mountain ranges look like small wrinkles on the planet's surface. But to us these mountains—some of which rise about six miles above sea level—seem gigantic. Our seas seem very deep, too. But the lowest known depth is only about seven miles.

Scientists believe the earth has a solid *inner core* with a temperature of about 9,000 degrees. Around this is a liquid *outer core* of mixed nickel and iron. A *mantle* of rock covers the earth's core. Each of these layers is many miles thick. Just below the earth's surface is the *crust,* a layer of rock just a few miles deep.

Some scientists believe the heat and pressure deep inside the earth's core make the outer layers rise or fall. They think these forces caused the first land to emerge from the sea in one huge chunk. They gave the name Pangaea to this first continent of ages past.

But the earth's top layer, or *crust,* was still very restless. In one especially big earthquake, perhaps, this huge piece of land broke apart in its weakest places. Very slowly, over many, many centuries, large chunks of land floated off from each other. Two large chunks joined by a narrow strip floated to the west, and became North and South America. The biggest chunk broke into three not-quite-separate pieces and floated to the East. It became Europe, Asia and Africa. A very large piece floated up and attached itself to the lower part of Asia, becoming the peninsula of India. Some scientists think this piece bumped the Asian coastline so hard that it pushed up land to form the tall Himalaya mountains.

Scientists have tried very hard to find out if this is really how the continents were formed. The best clue is the *shape* of the continents. The bulge of Africa seems to fit very well into the hollow of the Caribbean Sea between North and South America. And the bulge of South America looks as if it would fit into Africa's hollow just like a piece in a jigsaw puzzle.

This idea about how the continents were formed is called "continental drift." Not all scientists think it is true. But in some way, the land on earth came to look as it does today. A narrow land bridge connects the continents of North and South America. Europe, Asia, and Africa are connected, too. Only a mountain range called the Urals marks the boundary between Europe and Asia.

No matter how it happened, the lands of the earth were divided into definite parts, all quite different. Today many things make these land masses, or *continents,* very different from each other.

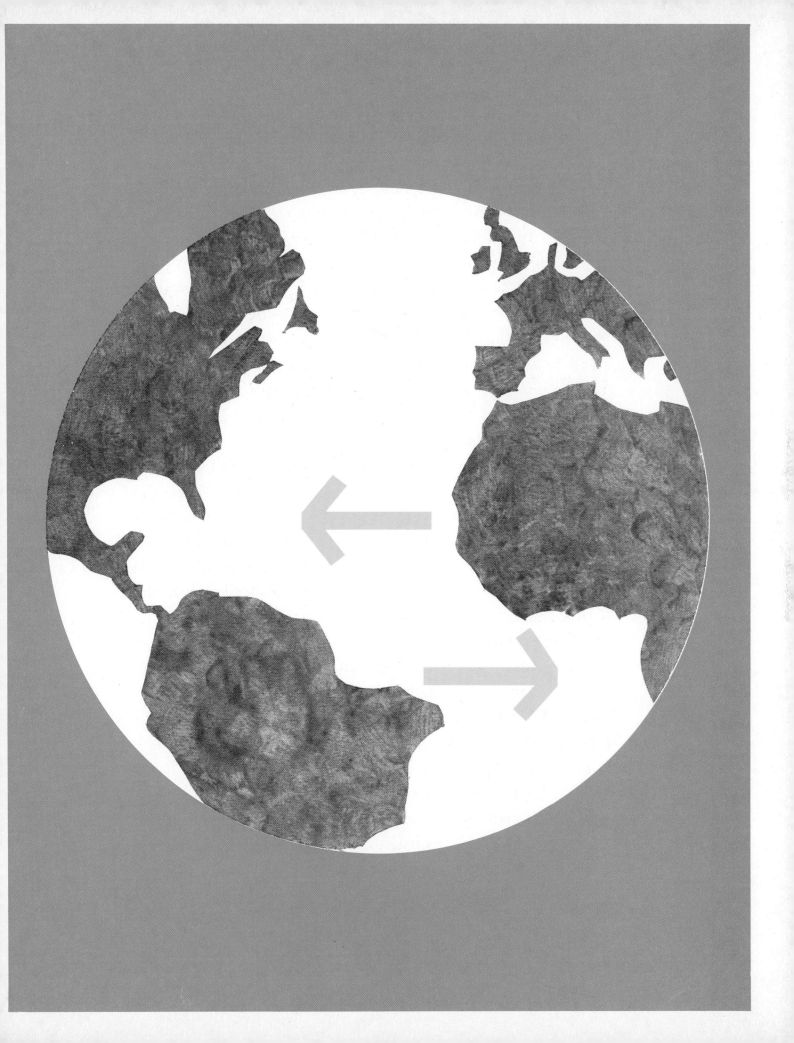

The Continents

ASIA IS THE BIGGEST continent on earth. Nearly half of all the people in the world live there. The name *Asia* makes most people think of rice and chop suey and pagodas and people who have yellow-brown skin and eat with chopsticks. But Asia is so big that these things are true about only some parts of it.

China has more people than any other country in the world. More than one billion people live there! In the north, the land of China is cold and dry and hilly. In the south there is hot, wet land, called *padi*, where people grow rice. China has some large cities with factories and stores and large buildings, but most of its people still live and work on farms.

Another large country of Asia is India. It is the big triangular peninsula on the southern part of the continent. India also has many millions of people, who belong to a different race than the Chinese and Japanese and other yellow-skinned Asian peoples.

The other very important country in Asia is Japan. It is on several small islands near the mainland of the continent. The Japanese must use every inch of their land, either to grow food or to make products that they can sell to other countries.

A kind of "land bridge" of many small countries and kingdoms connects the continents of Asia and Africa. These countries are often called "the Middle East." Their people are neither Asian nor African. Most are Arabs. The Middle East is mostly a land of low, flat deserts. There are only a few large cities, like Baghdad in Iraq, Damascus in Syria, Tehran in Iran, Tel Aviv in Israel, and Beirut in Lebanon.

Away from the seacoasts where most cities are, *Africa* has not changed much since ancient times. The countries of central Africa are very near the Equator, and so are hot most of the time. There are thick green rain forests where trees and ferns grow tall enough to block out the sunlight. Wild animals, bright-colored birds, and humming insects live in those jungles. Few people live here. Their small villages, with grass-roofed huts, are built beside the slow-moving rivers.

At the edges of the jungle are miles and miles of broad grasslands. There are no towns or roads here. Thousands of giraffes, zebras, and other animals roam these plains.

North Africa is very different from the steamy jungles and grasslands. Here there is desert, as far as you can see.

Though it is one of the smallest continents, *Europe* has been one of the most important in the history of

15

the world. After the great civilizations of Asia and the Middle East grew less important, Europe became the most powerful part of the world.

Most of the Mediterranean countries—Italy, Greece, Spain, and Portugal—are *peninsulas*. Water surrounds them on three sides. They are warm much of the time, but can be cool and rainy in the mountains and during the winter.

Furthest north in Europe are Sweden, Norway, and Denmark—the countries called *Scandinavia*—and Finland. The northern parts reach all the way to the Arctic. In summer, the "Midnight Sun" shines nearly all night long. Some parts of Scandinavia have steep mountains running down to the sea, with beautiful inlets called *fiords*.

The two largest countries in western Europe are France and Germany. They both have many different kinds of land and people—small farms, little towns, busy cities, thick forests, rugged mountains, and flat

farmland. The famous Alps mountains are in the center of Europe, mostly in the tiny country of Switzerland.

Eastern Europe includes the countries of Poland, Czechoslovakia, Hungary, Yugoslavia, and the eastern part of Germany. This part of Europe has rugged mountains, long rivers, and beautiful old cities like Budapest, Warsaw, and Prague.

The Soviet Union is both the easternmost country in Europe, and the easternmost and westernmost country in Asia. It has more land than any other country in the world. Because it is so big, Russia has many different kinds of lands and people.

In the 1400's the countries of Europe were rich and powerful. But the European kings wanted two things more—more land to rule over, and a better way to get to Asia. From Spain, Portugal, and England, explorers set out across the Atlantic ocean.

The land they found stretched all the way from the cold Arctic in the north to the cold Antarctic in the south.

In between were hot tropical lands, wide warm prairies, and cold mountains. There were two great continents—North and South America.

The western edge of *South America* is edged with the steep Andes mountains. There are many towns and cities in the warm, narrow strip of land between the mountains and the sea. On the eastern side of the mountains, much of the land is hot and tropical.

In some ways, central South America is like central Africa with thick green jungles and slow-moving rivers. Birds and monkeys skitter through the trees. The Amazon, the longest river in the world, runs through the heart of Brazil, the largest country in South America. Practically no one except the Indians who live there has explored this land.

Argentina, to the south, is the other large country. Its central plains are grasslands called *pampas*, where *gauchos* herd cattle like cowboys do in the United States.

Six small tropical countries make up the land bridge of Central America which connects South America to North America. These countries are warm all year

round, and bananas, palm trees, and colorful fruits and plants grow there. Across the narrowest part of Panama runs the famous Panama Canal.

North America has three countries—Canada, Mexico, and the United States. These neighbors are quite different from each other.

Mexico is more like South America, because they both were conquered and settled by Spanish soldiers. Like the United States, it had a revolution and became an independent country. A mountain range, the Sierra Madre, runs down its western coast, and in the mountains it is cool and dry. But the parts of Mexico on the seacoast—both on the east and the west—are tropical. Other parts are hot but very dry.

Canada is the largest country in the New World; only Russia has more land. The north, which stretches to the Arctic, is a thriving frontier. Highways and towns now dot a land once inhabited only by Eskimos. Eastern Canada is highly industrialized. Fertile farmlands fill the western prairies. West of the Rocky Mountains, big cities and colorful orchards line the warm Pacific coast.

19

Finally, there is the center of the North American continent — the United States. Along the eastern shore is a plain where the first settlers from England, Holland, and Sweden settled. The 13 colonies that became "united states" began here in the 1600's.

Next comes a sharp ridge of mountains that runs from Maine to Georgia. West of the mountains the country flattens out. There are rolling hills and flat prairies all the way to Colorado. In the plains states there are farms where corn and wheat and vegetables grow. There are dairy farms too.

The Rocky Mountains rise up near the western shore of the United States. The West has many other mountain ranges too. The United States, like any large country, has many different kinds of land. Some places are hot and tropical. Others are cool most of the year, with cold snowy winters.

But the United States probably has more different kinds of *people* than most other countries. They have come from Europe, from Asia, from Africa, and even from South America. People from all continents came to build this country in the New World.

Island Worlds

ISLANDS ARE A KIND of small world by themselves.
There is water all around an island—a river, a lake, or
an ocean. The only way you can get to an island is by a
boat, or an airplane, or sometimes a long bridge.

There are many islands all over the world, both big
and small. Some are just large enough for a few trees.
But others can hold millions of people and many busy
streets full of houses, cars, and skyscrapers. Much of
New York City is on three islands—Manhattan, Staten,
and Long islands. Venice, Italy, is on so many islands
that its streets are mostly canals! The island cities of

Hong Kong and Singapore, off the coast of Asia, are large seaports.

Some islands are so big that they can hold *many* big cities and many people. They are countries all by themselves. The British Isles are two big islands off the continent of Europe. One contains the countries of England, Scotland, and Wales. The other is Ireland.

Japan is a country built on islands that were once the tops of mountains. The four main islands are Honshu, Kyushu, Hokkaido, and Shikoku.

Many islands are rocky and mountainous. These are actually the *tops* of old mountains or volcanoes that sank into the sea, so that nothing shows above the water except the peaks. This is why many islands are long chains, like a string of beads. They are old mountain ranges.

The fiftieth state of the United States, Hawaii, is a chain of nine beautiful green islands that were once the peaks of volcanoes. Other volcanoes in the islands are still active.

OCEANIA

Between Australia and Southeast Asia, the southern Pacific ocean is so full of islands that it is sometimes called the "continent of Oceania." Once upon a time, millions of years ago, all this land was much higher, and a mountainous land bridge joined Australia to the continent. Then the land shifted and sank. The ocean flowed over much of the land, leaving the peaks and high places as dots of green land in the sea.

The huge jungle islands of Borneo, Java, Sumatra, and New Guinea were some of the largest parts left above water. Farther west are the three groups of islands called Polynesia, Micronesia, and Melanesia, separated by hundreds of miles of water. Famous islands like Samoa and Tahiti are here. They are the homes of the best sailors and navigators in the world — the Polynesians. Thousands of years before anyone in Europe or Africa had the courage to sail more than a few miles from shore, Polynesian sailors in huge outrigger canoes were sailing from island to island. They had no maps and no compasses, but they steered by the stars. Finally, several great canoes sailed most of the way across the Pacific, and the Polynesians became the first settlers of Hawaii.

At the southern tip of the watery continent of Oceania is the biggest island in the world — Australia. It is so large that it is usually listed in books as a continent. If you look for Australia on the globe, you can understand why people sometimes call it "Down Under."

Most of the other important islands of the world are fairly near something else. But Australia has been separated from Asia by the ocean for millions of years. So its plants and animals grew up to be quite a bit different from those in the lands closer together.

Australia has the *kangaroo*, who carries its babies in a pouch like an apron pocket. There's the *koala*, who lives in eucalyptus trees and looks very much like a teddy bear. Other Australian animals are just as unusual as their names — wombats, wallabies, dingos, and the duck-billed platypus! And these strange creatures live nowhere else in the world except Australia. (And in the zoo!)

Most of the people in Australia live near the coast in large cities like Melbourne, Sydney, and Brisbane. Other settlers live on flat plains where sheep or cattle graze on hundreds of miles of empty land. Ranches in Australia are so far apart that nearly everyone travels by airplane. Even doctors and nurses sometimes visit their patients by plane.

Granite, Glaciers, and Geology

SOME PARTS OF THE WORLD are flat, dry, sandy deserts. Others are rocky and mountainous. Still others are wide, rolling prairies where long grasses grow. The men who study all these different land shapes are called *geologists*. The study of rocks and earth and how mountains and prairies and valleys are formed is called *geology*.

Geologists try to find out why there are mountains in some places and flat plains in others, why lakes and rivers are where they are, and what forces move the earth.

The young earth, millions of years ago, was very restless. There were earthquakes and landslides. Some-

times parts of the rock would be squeezed and folded together, just like a piece of soft wool folded over and over. A long fold of land might make a new mountain range in what had been a prairie.

Geologists have figured out which mountain ranges are "new" and which ones are "old." Probably the oldest mountains in the United States are the Appalachians and the Smokies and other small mountain ranges near the Atlantic ocean. The newest mountains are the Rocky Mountains in Colorado and Montana.

Old mountains are more *weathered*. That word means what it sounds like: storm and winds and rain and dust and all kinds of weather have worn away parts of the rocks of the mountains. Old mountains are lower. Their tops are round, not peaked and jagged. Often they are covered by trees and grass.

New mountains are higher and not so worn down. They have jagged, rocky peaks. Trees seldom grow on these peaks, and snow covers the highest ones all year.

The other great forces that build mountains are deep inside the earth itself. The earth is not a solid ball of soil and rocks and pebbles and boulders. Deep in the earth—deeper than the deepest parts of the sea—the earth is not solid at all. It is so unbelievably hot there that rocks melt! They become sticky, like thick taffy. And they are red hot.

Near the surface of the earth there are sometimes weak spots. In some places the earth's crust is thin. Sometimes the earth slides, and causes earthquakes. Whenever anything happens that makes it possible for the red-hot underground rocks to spurt out, a volcano is formed. Red-hot, liquid rock, called *lava*, flows from a crack in the earth. Sometimes there are explosions, and rocks are tossed high into the air. Ashes, rocks, and lava build up a cone-shaped mountain. Many mountains of today are old volcanoes that do not erupt any more. The Cascade range near the Pacific coast in California is made of old volcanoes.

Volcanoes still erupt in many parts of the world. During our century, several large volcanoes have erupted. Whole cities have been buried by ashes and lava. Many thousands of people have been killed. When Krakatoa, a volcano in Indonesia, erupted in 1883, it killed 36,000 people. The sound of the explosion was heard 3,000 miles away. So much ash and dirt were thrown into the air that there were colorful sunsets all over the world for a year afterward.

One of the most famous volcanoes — Mt. Vesuvius — erupted almost 1900 years ago. It completely buried two little towns, Pompeii and Herculaneum, with ash and soot and lava. People eventually forgot that the towns had ever existed. When the towns were discovered many years afterward, they were almost exactly the way they had been when Vesuvius blew up. Dishes were sitting on the tables in houses. Bread was on the counters in the bakery. The eruption of Vesuvius had stopped everything in just a few minutes.

Only a few volcanoes are building mountains today. But when the earth was younger, millions of years ago, there were many of these fiery mountains. They built mountain ranges and islands all over the world.

THE CHANGING SURFACE OF EARTH

Volcanoes and earthquakes change the surface of the earth. Many other forces also change the land so that it looks the way it does. Water and weather do much to change the land. After mountains are built, running water carves them into hills and valleys. The Grand Canyon is miles and miles of colorful rock carved into a canyon that is more than a mile deep. At the bottom of the canyon is the tiny Colorado river. Though it is

hard to believe, that little river carved the huge canyon out of flat prairie land.

Other rivers, like the Mississippi, pick up dirt and rocks from along their banks and carry them downstream. At the mouths of the rivers, the dirt drops to the bottom, and new land called a *delta* is built.

Sometimes running water and falling water do great damage. They carry away the land where plants grow, and cut deep gullies. When wind and water ruin the land, the damage is called *erosion*.

Most of the water that changes the earth is running water—falling rain and the water that runs in creeks and rivers. But several million years ago, the earth had a long, long winter. Much of the water on earth froze, and became great flat sheets of ice called *glaciers*. Those long-ago glaciers moved mountains, leveled prairies, and dug giant lakes.

The glaciers in North America drifted slowly down from northern Canada. They covered nearly all of the northern half of the United States, as far south as what is now southern Illinois. These glaciers were huge sheets of ice, stretching for hundreds of miles, and almost a mile thick. They slid very slowly across the land.

The glaciers flattened out the flat prairies of the Dakotas, and the rolling plains country in Iowa and Illinois and Minnesota. As the glaciers melted, water filled five of the biggest ditches it had scooped out. These are the five Great Lakes. The glaciers made hundreds of smaller lakes, too.

At the edges of the glaciers the ice melted a little. The rocks and earth that the glaciers scooped off fell to the ground and formed ridges and oddly shaped hills. Giant boulders were dropped in fields many miles from where they had been picked up.

Compared with the other things that have changed the earth, glaciers came only a short time ago. Geologists think the last ones melted back about 11,000 years ago. Most of the other things geologists study happened millions and billions of years ago. So 11,000 years ago is practically yesterday!

There are still a few glaciers and ice sheets in the world today. Antarctica, the land around the South Pole, is covered by a great ice sheet ten miles thick in places. There are ice sheets near the North Pole, too. And there are smaller valley glaciers in many of the mountains of the world. They are still at work carving mountains.

Geologists think that we are just at the end of a great Ice Age. Unless something very unusual happens to the world's weather, there will not be another Ice Age for thousands of years. But the forces that change the land are still at work. The earth's surface is slowly changing all the time.

Water, Wind, and Weather

EVERYONE ON EARTH lives at the bottom of a great "sea" of air—the atmosphere around the earth. The atmosphere is made up of oxygen, other gases, little specks of dust—and *water*. Only a very little bit of all the water in the world is in the atmosphere. Most of the water is in the oceans. Yet water in the air is one of the most important things in giving us the kind of weather we have.

Sometimes the air loses a lot of its water, and then *rain* or *snow* falls. Sometimes the water collects around little specks of dust in the air and makes *clouds*.

Water from lakes, rivers, and oceans—and even little puddles—is constantly *evaporating*. It becomes *water vapor* and rises into the air. The air carries this water vapor to somewhere else. When the water vapor *condenses*, or turns back into water, it may fall as rain. It may freeze, and then it falls as snow. The rainfall and melting snow soak into the ground, or flow into rivers and creeks that carry them back to the lakes and oceans. There the water evaporates again, and rises into the air.

Weathermen have special names for the different kinds of clouds we see in the sky. The big piles of cottony clouds that move across the summer sky are called *cumulus*. Flat, streaky layers of clouds are called *stratus*. The high, wispy bits of clouds are named *cirrus*. These feathery clouds are so high in the sky that they are frozen. Cirrus clouds are made of ice crystals, not water droplets.

One kind of cumulus cloud almost always means a storm is coming. It is a high, flat-topped pile of clouds that seems to sit right on the horizon and tower into the sky. Sometimes people call such a cloud a *thunderhead*.

Another thing that is important in giving us the kind of weather we have is *wind*. Wind is air that is moving very fast. The air is always moving, no matter how quiet it may seem.

Winds are named for *where* they blow from most of the time. At the far north and far south, around the North and South Poles, the *polar winds* blow. They are icy cold, because they come from lands where there is ice and snow all year round. When cold, cold air blows from the polar zones, nearby parts of the world will have cold weather.

Around the Equator are two belts of *trade winds*. These are hot, dry winds that blow toward the Equator.

The winds that blow most of the time around the central areas of earth's two hemispheres are very important because they affect such a large part of the world. They are called *prevailing winds* because they blow in one direction most of the time. The prevailing winds are caused by the earth's spinning round and round, once each day.

In the northern hemisphere, the lands north of the Equator, the prevailing winds are *westerlies*. They blow from west to east. In the southern hemisphere, they are *prevailing easterlies*. They blow from east to west.

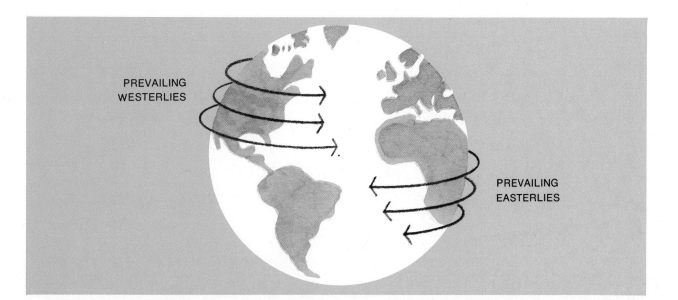

PREVAILING WESTERLIES

PREVAILING EASTERLIES

When the prevailing winds blow across huge oceans like the Atlantic or the Pacific, they pick up great amounts of water vapor. By the time they reach the western coasts of the big continents, the winds are very, very wet. As soon as they reach the land, they rise in the air — and drop most of their water as rain. If there are mountains along the coast, nearly all of the water in the air is dropped on the coastward side of the mountain range. The coasts of California, Washington, and Oregon in the United States get much rain brought by prevailing westerlies. So do England and the western shores of Europe.

In the southern hemisphere, it is the east coasts that are very rainy. The jungle of Brazil in South America is tropical rain forest watered by rain from prevailing easterly winds.

When the prevailing winds have blown over the coast areas, they continue inland, but they have very little water left in them. This is why the central parts of very large continents may be fairly dry grasslands or prairies, or even very dry deserts.

Much of the world's weather is caused by *local* winds and masses of warm or cold air that move across the land. Weathermen trace the paths of these air masses when they figure out the weather forecast for the next few days. Have you seen a weatherman on television draw lines and circles on the weather map? These show what storms or air masses are moving toward you.

Some strong storm winds have special names. *Tornadoes* are whirling, funnel-shaped wind clouds that can damage towns and buildings. They usually form in flat prairie country, where there are no hills or trees to break the wind. *Hurricanes* are violent storms that blow off the ocean. They often do great damage to towns near the coast and to ships at sea.

Weathermen use weather balloons to learn about conditions high in the sky, and they use weather satellites to find out where storms are. A weather satellite can take pictures of almost the whole United States, showing exactly where storms are and where they are moving. Weathermen also use instruments to measure temperature and humidity.

The *temperature* reading tells how hot or cold the air is. The thermometer used in the United States measures heat and cold in degrees Fahrenheit. We say that 32 degrees Fahrenheit is freezing temperature—water turns to ice, and water in the air turns to hail or snow. In many other countries, and in most scientific laboratories, a different temperature scale, called Celsius or Centigrade, is used. Nowadays we are beginning to use thermometers that measure heat and cold in degrees Celsius. We say that 0 degrees Celsius is the freezing point of water. Celsius is the scale that most scientists use to record temperature.

Humidity is the measure of how much water there is in the air. Warm air can hold much more water than cold air. When the wind hits a mountain range, it is forced higher into the air where it is cooler. Rain falls because the cooler air can no longer hold all its water.

Sometimes on very hot summer days, the air feels as though you could wring it out like a wet sponge. This means that the humidity is very high, probably over 90 per cent. If the humidity goes higher, you can expect rain. A "relative humidity" of 100 per cent means that the air is holding all the water it can. If the temperature drops, the cooler air will not be able to hold so much water, and rain will probably fall.

What Ancient People Thought About Space

THROUGHOUT THE AGES man has wondered about the sky. It is easy to understand why, since there is so much to see in it. Some ancient people worshipped the sun as a powerful god. They even built great temples to it, and they offered human sacrifices to the sun. And the stars, some people believed, were stuck to a huge dome. The earth was flat, they thought, and the dome was somehow attached to the ends of the earth.

It has taken men thousands of years to learn what we now know about the heavens. Today, much of what the ancient people thought about space seems ridiculous.

Yet they were trying to understand and explain the fascinating story of the heavens.

Ancient people began to study the sun, moon, stars and planets thousands of years before the birth of Christ. This study is the science we call *astronomy*.

Ancient people tried to explain what they saw in the skies. Some Chinese said that the Milky Way galaxy was steam from the breath of a huge elephant who lay submerged to his neck in the water of the skies. Some Greeks believed that the Milky Way was the main road through heaven. In Egypt, some people said that it was formed by kernels of corn dropped by the goddess Isis.

Ancient people felt that certain groups of stars made pictures in the sky. They named the groups after what the pictures looked like—Taurus the Bull, Aries the Ram, Pisces the Fish. These pictures in the sky are what we call *constellations*.

Ancient people used the stars and constellations to guide them at night. And they believed that the stars and constellations were responsible for much of what happened on Earth. Any strange event in the sky frightened them. A comet or a meteor was viewed with great fear by the people. A planet entering a certain constellation would suggest that some fearful or disastrous event was to take place on Earth.

These beliefs remained for thousands of years. In the year 1524, over 30 years after America was discovered, people all over the civilized world saw a terrible sign in the skies. Three planets — Mars, Jupiter and Saturn — came together in the constellation of Pisces the Fish. People believed this meant a great flood would cover the Earth. Many stopped their normal work and frantically built boats and arks. The flood, of course, never came.

41

The most common belief in ancient times was that the Earth was the center of the universe. In China, however, some astronomers held that the North Star, which we call *Polaris* or Pole Star, was the center. An ancient Greek astronomer named Aristarchus said the Earth revolved around the sun, but few people were willing to accept this idea.

The most famous of the early astronomers was a man named Ptolemy who lived in Egypt over 1,850 years ago. He wrote a book called the *Almagest* in which he "proved" that everything in the heavens revolved around the Earth. For the next 1,400 years, most people believed Ptolemy's idea.

It was not until the great age of astronomers in the 1500's and 1600's that Ptolemy's idea was corrected. Copernicus and Galileo started men on the right track to understanding the universe by explaining that the earth and other planets revolve around the sun. Other great astronomers like Tycho Brahe, Johann Kepler, Isaac Newton and Edmund Halley added still more to our understanding of the heavenly bodies.

Our Sun

OUR SUN IS a faithful friend. Every morning it rises in the east, often long before we get out of bed. It slowly lights up the sky. The darkness of night disappears.

Even on a cloudy morning when we cannot see the sun at all, it gives off enough light to let us know that it is daytime. We can be absolutely certain that every morning the sun will be there. Our faithful sun has not missed a day since the world began. And it never will as long as our world exists.

The sun really doesn't *rise*. It seems to come up in the east, and to travel slowly across the sky until it passes out of sight in the west each night. What really happens is that the Earth, our planet, is rotating. It is spinning around like a top. In the morning when we first see the sun, the part of the Earth where we live is turning toward the sun. The Earth continues to turn, and gradually the part where we live turns away from the sun. Then we have night. Each 24 hours the sun appears again.

Even thousands of years ago, ancient people knew how important the sun was. Many of them worshipped it as a god. Some Egyptians thought the sun was a bright, fiery ship that sailed across the sky each day, or a great ball of fire pushed by a beetle!

The ancient people of Greece told a story about how hot the sun was. A clever man named Daedalus made two pairs of wings so that he and his son could fly away from their enemies. But his son Icarus was foolish and flew too close to the sun. The sun was so hot that it melted the wax which held his wings on. Poor Icarus fell into the sea.

This story, of course, is a *myth,* a story like a fairy tale. But even if Icarus could fly, he could not fly very close to the sun. The sun is about 93 million miles away from the Earth. If he flew at 60 miles per hour without ever stopping, it would have taken him approximately 177 years to reach the sun.

And the sun is very much hotter than the ancient Greeks thought it was. We think it is hot here on Earth when the temperature reaches 90 degrees. The temperature on the surface of the sun is about 10,000 degrees. And inside the sun at its *core,* the temperature is over 27 million degrees.

If the sun is so hot, why doesn't it just burn up? After all, it is much hotter than any fire or heat here on Earth.

It is important to understand that the sun is not a ball of fire, although it may look like one. Also, the sun is not solid like the Earth or the moon. It is made up of

gases. One type of gas on the sun is *hydrogen*. Through a nuclear reaction, hydrogen gas changes into helium gas. When this happens tremendous heat is created. This nuclear reaction goes on all the time, and so the sun remains a glowing ball of intense heat.

The sun is a place of tremendous action too. Violent explosions shake its surface. From deep inside the sun, hot gases called *flares* burst through the sun's surface. Streams of hot gases leap out like great torches. Some of these streamers reach out a hundred thousand miles and then fall back into the sun. Cooler gases form dark spots on the sun, which are called *sunspots*. Sunspots may last only a few hours or for as long as two months. Their temperature is much lower than the area around them.

Like all of the other stars, the sun is moving. In fact, nothing in the universe is standing still. The sun rotates on its own axis. At the same time, it moves through space carrying the Earth and the other planets right along with it.

Our sun is a star, like many of the other stars in the sky. It only looks different, because it is so much closer to us. The other stars are billions of miles farther away. Most of them are so far away we cannot even see them without a telescope. But most of them are suns, much like our sun. They, too, produce heat, light and energy.

Our sun is very large. More than one million planets the size of our Earth would fit inside it. Yet our sun is only an average-size star. There are many stars which are much brighter. Others are hundreds of times larger. Still, to us, it is the most important star in the universe.

Our Moon

THE TWO MEN, dressed in heavy, awkward space suits, moved with slow, loping steps. The dark landscape behind them was barren of all life. For long moments, people around the world watched the strange scene on their television sets in amazement. Was man actually walking on the surface of the moon? Was the incredible event really being seen live back on Earth? As Neil Armstrong, the first man to walk on the moon, said, this was indeed "one giant leap for mankind."

The landing on the Sea of Tranquility in 1969 proved that man can survive in an environment vastly

47

different from Earth's. Properly dressed and equipped, Armstrong and his *Apollo XI* crewmate, Edwin Aldrin, were not greatly hindered in their movements. The low gravity on the moon made walking difficult, but not impossible.

Armstrong and Aldrin were able to set down their lunar module, *Eagle,* set up several scientific experiments, and collect rock and soil samples. Crews from later Apollo flights have brought back rock and soil samples from other areas of the moon's surface. Scientists are studying these samples to find out what the moon is made of, how old it is, and how it was formed.

Russian spacecraft have also explored the moon's surface. *Luna XIV,* an unmanned spacecraft, landed on the moon in 1970. It brought back moon dust samples. Later that year, the Russians landed a self-propelled vehicle, called *Lunokhod,* on the moon. As it traveled across the moon's surface, the eight-wheeled research craft analyzed soil and rock contents and transmitted this information back to Russian space scientists. Lunokhod's movements were controlled from Earth.

Men have been studying the moon for hundreds of years. The fact that the moon travels around the Earth was discovered by an Italian astronomer named Galileo Galilei, who lived about 350 years ago. Galileo built a small telescope, and with it he was able to look out into space and see things that no man had ever seen before.

The telescope was a wonderful invention. It allowed man to study closely all of the heavenly bodies—the moon, planets, the sun and the stars. Telescopes allow us to see things which we could not see with just our eyes. Scientists through the years have created better and better telescopes. The telescopes scientists use today are much better than the one that Galileo used.

Another thing that helped scientists learn more about the moon was the invention of rockets and missiles. With these powerful vehicles, men launched satellites around the Earth. Later, spacecraft were built that could go even farther and orbit the moon. And finally

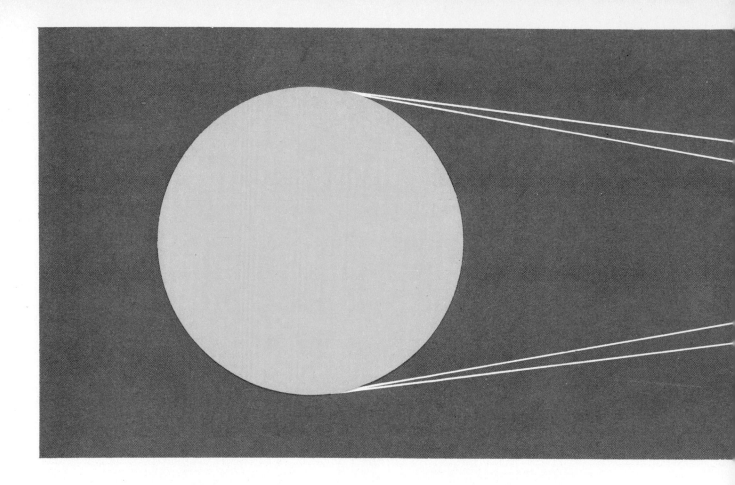

rockets which could land on the moon were developed.

With the telescope and other wonderful inventions, men learned exactly how far away the moon is and how large it is. The moon is usually about 238,000 miles from the Earth. At certain times it is over 253,000 miles away. At other times it is closer, only a little over 221,000 miles away. A trip to the moon is the same as traveling from New York to San Francisco 80 times without stopping.

Space probes sending back pictures of the moon's surface showed that it differed from the Earth in many ways. On the moon there are only mountains, craters and valleys. They are covered with rocks and dust.

The moon has no water and no air. The air that surrounds our Earth—the same air we breathe—is called our *atmosphere*. The moon has no atmosphere. Because it

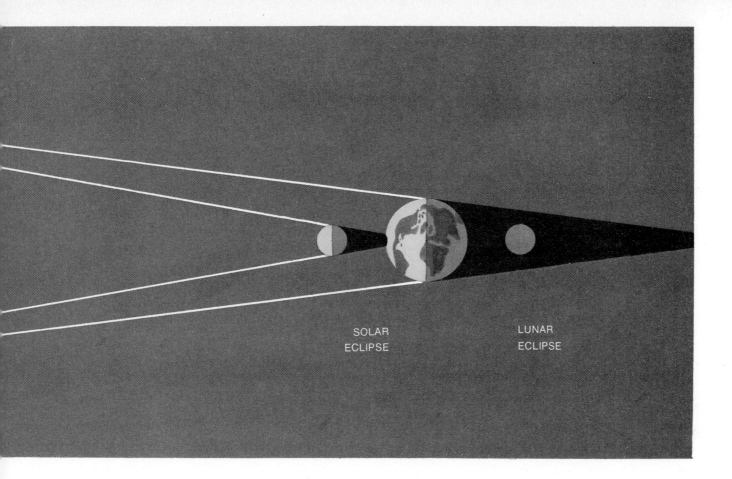

SOLAR
ECLIPSE

LUNAR
ECLIPSE

has no atmosphere, the moon has no clouds, no wind, and no rain or snow. Because there is no air on the moon, astronauts wear helmets which completely cover their heads, and space suits which cover their bodies. Air is pumped into the helmets from tanks brought with them from Earth.

Each "day" and each "night" on the moon is two weeks long. Daytime temperatures on the moon are usually about 214 degrees. This is hot enough to boil water. Nighttime temperatures may go down to 243 degrees below zero. The coldest temperature ever recorded on Earth is only about 127 degrees below zero.

To us on Earth the moon always seems to be changing its shape. Sometimes we see a round full moon, sometimes a half-moon, and sometimes a sliver of a moon. Some nights we can see no moon at all.

Half of the moon is always lighted by the sun, but we do not always see all the lighted half. How much of the lighted half we see depends on where the moon is in its orbit around the Earth.

As it travels around the Earth, the moon sometimes passes between the sun and the Earth and blots out the light of the sun. This is called a *solar eclipse*. Ancient people used to be terrified when a solar eclipse occurred. There are times, too, when the moon is on the other side of the Earth. Then, the Earth is between the sun and the moon, and the Earth blocks off the light from the sun. When this happens the Earth casts its shadow across the moon, causing a *lunar eclipse*.

The moon is certainly not a pleasant place to visit. Why then do people go to all the trouble of sending astronauts there? There are really many reasons.

For one thing, there may be valuable minerals on the moon, like gold, uranium, iron or nickel. Another reason is that we can study the stars and planets much more easily from the moon because the moon has no atmosphere. Telescopes on the moon would give us much clearer views of the stars and planets than they do from Earth. From the moon we would probably be able to predict the weather on Earth much better. It would be possible to see giant storms taking shape halfway around the world.

The most exciting thing about reaching the moon is the future. Perhaps one day a space station will be built there. Spaceships launched from this station would explore other planets. The moon is only a first step in our exploration of the universe.

The Planets

"THE EARTH IS NOT the center of the universe," said the famous astronomer Nicolas Copernicus. "We have been wrong. It is really the Earth that revolves around the sun."

Copernicus suggested this astonishing idea in the early 1500's. For thousands of years people had believed that everything in the heavens revolved around the Earth. Copernicus knew that people were not ready to accept his startling idea, which would upset many religious beliefs. So he wrote it in a book that he did not allow to be published until after his death.

Copernicus was right, of course, about people not being ready to believe him. Many years would pass before people would accept his idea.

Today, we know that the Earth is only one of nine planets which all revolve around our sun. We call the sun and the planets that go around it our *solar system*. Our solar system includes the sun and everything that revolves around it — planets, moons, comets, meteors and asteroids. But the planets are the most important.

On a clear night, we can sometimes see some of the planets. Planets reflect light from our sun, just as the moon does. Because the planets are much nearer to us than any of the stars, they usually look bigger and brighter than the stars.

We know of nine planets in our solar system. There may be others which have not yet been located. In fact, the last planet to be discovered, Pluto, was not found until 1930.

The planets do not move around the sun in a perfect circle. They move in an *ellipse*, which is sort of a stretched-out circle.

Copernicus said that in addition to traveling around the sun, each planet also turns on its own *axis*. This is another way of saying that each planet spins like a top as it moves around the sun.

Why do the planets stay in their orbits around the sun? Why don't they fly off into space? A famous English astronomer named Isaac Newton found the explanation. It is a force we call *gravity*. Newton said that everything is pulled toward something else. The bigger and closer an object is, the more power it has in drawing things toward it. The Earth is the biggest and closest thing to us who live on it. Therefore, it pulls us toward it. We do not float off into space. We throw a ball into the air and it falls back to Earth. It is drawn back by the force of gravity.

In our solar system, the biggest object is the sun. It draws the Earth and all the other planets toward it. Why aren't we pulled into the sun, then? The answer is because we are whirling around the sun.

If you tie a ball on a string and swing it around in a circle, it stays in the air and feels as if it is trying to pull away from you. This pulling-away feeling is called *centrifugal* force. The Earth and the planets are swinging around the sun much like balls on the ends of strings. Gravity— the pulling-in power of the sun—keeps the planets from whirling off into space. Centrifugal force—the pulling-away power of the whirling planets—keeps the planets from being drawn into the sun. The two forces work against each other to keep us orbiting around the sun.

Mercury, the planet closest to the sun, is also one of the smallest. It takes Mercury only 88 days to make a complete orbit around the sun. That means Mercury's

MERCURY

VENUS

EARTH

year is only 88 days long. But Mercury makes only one turn on its axis every 88 days. Therefore, one side of Mercury is always facing the sun. It is tremendously hot. Scientists think it is about 660 degrees on the daylight side of Mercury. The other side is always facing away from the sun. It is always very cold, more than 200 degrees below zero.

Venus is the planet closest to the Earth. At one point in its orbit, it is only 25 million miles from the Earth. Venus is about the same size as the Earth, and takes 225 days to orbit the sun. Venus is surrounded by thick clouds that make it impossible to see the planet. Soviet and American space probes have found Venus to be dry and very hot—about 800 degrees. This planet is among the brightest and most beautiful sights in the sky.

Earth is certainly the most important planet to us. It is our home. Earth is a medium-sized planet. It travels around the sun once in 365 days, which is how we

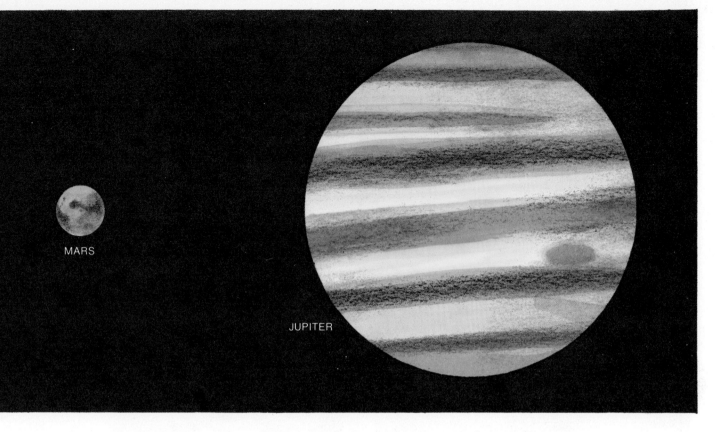

MARS

JUPITER

determine our year. And it rotates on its axis once every 24 hours (a day). To us, the Earth seems a very big place, but in the universe, it is only a tiny speck.

Mars is the next farthest planet out beyond Earth. Mars takes 687 days to revolve around the sun. It has a bright red glow, and can be seen easily from the Earth. Through a telescope, astronomers can see light and dark patches on Mars. It was once thought that the light areas were deserts and the dark areas were seas. But scientists now believe that there is probably no flowing water on Mars. Space ships have sent back pictures which seem to show that Mars is a dry, dusty place like the moon.

Jupiter is the largest planet, though it is still much smaller than our sun. This giant planet is about 1500 times as big as our Earth, and has many moons! Through a telescope, patches and spots can be seen on Jupiter. Some astronomers think these may be clouds. It takes Jupiter almost 12 of our Earth years to orbit around the sun.

SATURN

URANUS

Saturn is one of the most unusual of the planets because it has three rings which encircle it. The rings vary in brightness. They also cast shadows on the planet itself. The rings seem to be made of millions of small meteors or other tiny particles. Each particle is probably no bigger than a small stone. Saturn is the second largest planet in our solar system. Its orbit around the sun takes nearly 30 Earth years.

Uranus was not discovered until 1781. It is smaller than Jupiter or Saturn but still much larger than the Earth. Uranus is difficult to see because it is so far away. It takes this planet 84 Earth years to orbit the sun!

Neptune cannot be seen without a telescope. It is slightly smaller than Uranus, but is still one of the giant

58

NEPTUNE

PLUTO

planets. Neptune is tremendously cold because it is so far away from the sun. In fact, the warmest it gets on Neptune is 360 degrees below zero. It takes Neptune 164 Earth years to travel once around the sun.

Pluto is the farthest planet we know about. We think it is also the smallest. Pluto was not discovered until 1930. Some scientists believe that it is not a planet at all. They think it is perhaps one of Neptune's moons. Pluto takes over 247 years to orbit the sun. It is a bitterly cold, desolate planet, so far away that we have been able to learn very little about it. Pluto is so far from the Earth that light from it takes over five hours to reach us. If Pluto suddenly blew up, we would not know it on Earth until five hours later.

Comets, Meteors, and Asteroids

COMETS ARE AMONG the most exciting things in the sky. Some travel swiftly through the sky streaming a bright fiery tail behind them.

Before people knew much about comets, they were afraid of these strange visitors in the heavens. People thought that the appearance of a comet meant some terrible tragedy would happen on Earth. We know today that this is not true at all. A comet is simply another neighbor of ours in space.

Comets usually make a wide orbit around the sun. Their orbit is an *ellipse*, like that of the planets, but

it is much longer. At one end of the comet's orbit is the sun, and at the other end usually one of the large planets like Jupiter or Neptune. As it approaches the sun a comet moves much faster, because the sun's tremendous force of *gravity* pulls it faster.

A comet with a tail is easy to spot. However, most comets do not have tails. As comets approach the sun, some will form a tail. The closer the comet gets to the sun, the longer the tail becomes. Some comet tails are millions of miles long. As the comet passes around the sun and heads back out into space, the tail gets smaller and smaller until it finally disappears.

The tail of a comet always points away from the sun. This is because the pressure from the sun pushes gases and dust away from the head of the comet. The tail is simply the gases and dust trailing behind.

61

Comets are very light in weight. In fact, the Earth is about a million times heavier than the heaviest comet. No one knows for sure what comets are made of. They are probably loose clumps of gases, dust and small rocks.

One of the most famous comets is Halley's comet. It is named after the astronomer who discovered it, Edmund Halley. It appears in the sky about every 75 years. Some comets, however, appear only every thousand years or more. Halley's comet last was seen from Earth in 1910. It is scheduled to visit the Earth again in 1986.

Meteors are another interesting sight in the sky. They are often called "shooting stars" because they make a bright flash, racing across the sky. But they are not stars. Stars do not fall or shoot across the sky.

Meteors are chunks of stone or iron. They vary in size from a tiny speck of dust to large boulders weighing several tons. But all meteors are too small to see when they are in outer space. When a meteor enters the Earth's atmosphere, it becomes tremendously hot as it rushes through the air. The meteor becomes a white-hot glowing ball speeding toward the Earth. The brightest meteors are called *fireballs*. They are so bright they seem to light up the entire sky. If it is a large meteor, small chunks may break off and trail behind it. When this happens, the stream of bright pieces trailing behind the meteor looks like a fireworks display.

After a meteor has fallen to Earth, it is called a *meteorite*. Most meteorites are very small, but a few large ones have been found. The largest was discovered in Africa, and weighed almost 60 tons. Meteor Crater in

Arizona is believed to have been caused by the crash of a meteor. The crater is three-fourths of a mile wide and almost 600 feet deep!

Most meteors burn up completely before they reach the Earth. But still, about 2,000 large meteors strike the Earth each year.

Asteroids are chunks of stone or iron like meteors, but they are much larger. Even though we call them the "little planets," they are much smaller than even the smallest planet. Asteroids come in all shapes and sizes. Some are fairly round like the planets. Others are rugged and resemble a huge boulder. One called *Eros* looks like a giant loaf of bread.

Each asteroid revolves around the sun in its own orbit. Practically all of them are between the orbits of Mars and Jupiter. Only one asteroid, named *Vesta*, can be seen without a telescope. The others are too small and too far away.

We do not know how the asteroids came to be. Some scientists think that they were created at the same time and in the same way as the planets. Others believe that there was once a planet between Mars and Jupiter. This planet either exploded or collided with some other huge body in space. The shattered pieces of planet are what we call asteroids.

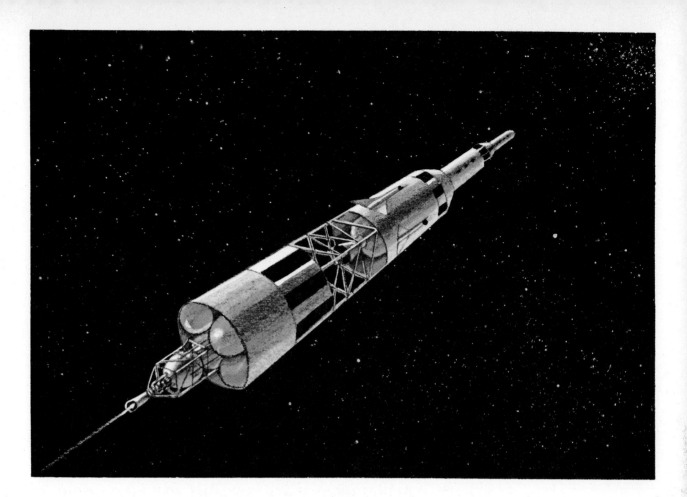

Among the Stars

SUPPOSE THAT THERE IS LIFE on a planet which revolves around a star far away from the Earth. Suppose someone there wants to send us a letter to tell us that there is life on that planet. He would have to address his letter something like this:

> Mr. David Johnson
> 1516 N. Main Street
> Chicago, Illinois, U. S. A.
> The Earth
> The Solar System
> The Milky Way Galaxy
> The Universe

Suppose, too, that the Post Office on his planet can send letters at the speed of light, which is 186,000 miles per second. That means that the letter would travel 16,070,400,000 miles in a day. But even traveling at this incredible rate of speed, the letter would not reach us on Earth for hundreds of millions of *years*. That is how far away some of the stars are from the Earth.

Our sun is a star, too. It looks different from other stars simply because it is so much closer to us. But it is only one of trillions of stars in the sky.

Our sun-star is part of a *system* of stars called a *galaxy*. Our galaxy is known as the Milky Way galaxy because the part of it that we can see from Earth looks like a great milky ribbon spread across the night sky. There are more than a hundred billion stars in our Milky Way galaxy.

If we were able to stand back and look at the whole Milky Way galaxy, it would look like a huge pinwheel. It is flat, like a wheel, but bulging in the center as if it has hubcaps. Two long arms of the pinwheel trail out from the center. There are billions of stars in our galaxy, and all of them are constantly in motion. Our galaxy is like a tremendous wheel turning in space.

Our sun is about 35,000 *light years* from the center of the Milky Way galaxy. That means if you were traveling through space at 186,000 miles per second (the speed of light), it would take you 35,000 years to reach the center of our galaxy. Our sun—together with its planets, comets, asteroids, and meteors—is on one of the huge arms streaming out from the center of the galaxy. The distance from one side of the Milky Way galaxy all the way across to the other side is over 80,000 light years.

As huge as our galaxy is, it is by no means the only one in the universe. There are at least a hundred million other galaxies. Probably there are many, many more which we cannot see because our telescopes are not powerful enough. Many of the other galaxies we can see are much larger than ours.

Many stars, too, are larger than our sun, and many are brighter. In fact, our sun is only an average star in size and brightness. Some stars are large enough to put almost half of our solar system inside them.

We can tell about the *heat* of a star by its color. The "hottest" are blue stars and white stars. Average stars are yellow. The coldest stars are red. We also describe stars by their size—these sizes are super-giant, giant, or dwarf. Our sun is yellow, which means it is medium hot, and is classified as a giant star.

Some stars are really *double stars* or *star clusters*. They sometimes look like just a single star. But when we look through a telescope we find that there are two or even more stars. A star cluster may be several stars which are not close together at all, but are simply in the same line of sight. Or it may be several stars which are close together, making up their own system. The most famous star clusters are the Pleiades, sometimes called the Seven Sisters, and the Gemini Twins.

Out among the stars, there are also *nebulae*. These are great clouds of gas. There are different kinds of nebulae. A *planetary nebula* is a huge mass of gas which surrounds a star. There is also a *gaseous nebula*, which is a thin cloud of gas that appears as a bright object in the sky. A *dark nebula*, which looks like a hole in the sky, is really a mass of gases and other material located between us and stars out beyond it. A dark nebula blocks our view of other stars and appears as a dark blot in the sky.

We often think of the stars as only being out at night. The stars, of course, are there all the time. We can see them only at night. During the day the light from our own sun is so bright we cannot see any of the other stars.

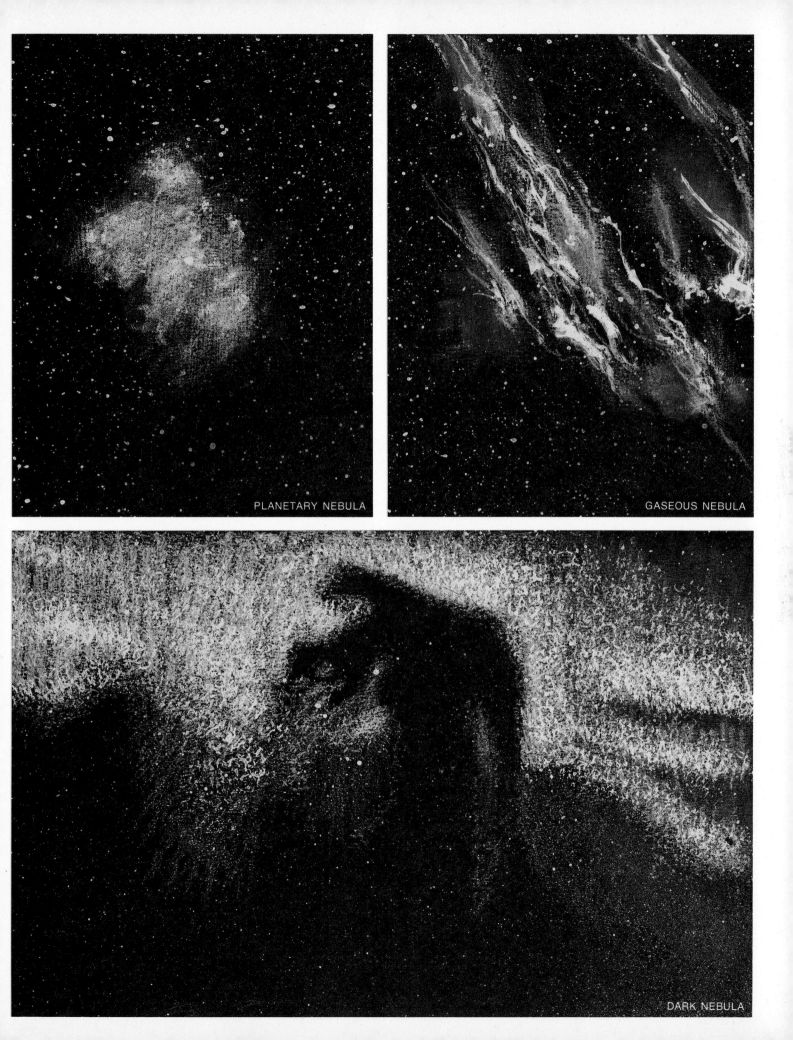

PLANETARY NEBULA

GASEOUS NEBULA

DARK NEBULA

Even though our sun is by far the most important star to us on Earth, the other stars are helpful. Travelers for centuries used them to find their way at night. Ships and even airplanes have used stars to help them navigate.

People in the southern hemisphere of Earth do not see the same stars as people in the northern hemisphere. They look out on a different section of the sky, one which people in the northern hemisphere never see. The brightest star in the northern skies is Sirius, but it cannot be seen from Australia or Argentina. On the other hand, the brightest star in the southern skies is Canopus, which cannot be seen in the north. The most famous constellation in that part of the world is the Southern Cross.

Rockets and Missiles

ALTHOUGH POWERFUL ROCKETS for space exploration are new, man has known how to make simple rockets for hundreds of years.

In the year 1232, the Chinese used rockets in battle. The rockets were attached to sticks and fired from the ground. They were called "arrows of fire."

Over 200 years later, an Italian named Joanes de Fontana designed other rockets for war. His plan was to equip the rockets with rollers or wheels and disguise them as rabbits, fish and birds. They were supposed to roll across the battlefield and terrify the enemy.

About the year 1500, a Chinese named Wan Hoo became the first man to try to use rockets as a form of travel. He gathered 47 of the largest rockets available and attached them to the back of a chair. A kite was placed on each side of the chair. Wan Hoo sat in the chair and signalled his helpers to ignite the 47 rockets. They carefully lit the fuses and then retreated a safe distance. In a huge blast of noise and flame, Wan Hoo and his "rocket-chair" became the first casualty in man's attempt to soar into outer space.

As the years passed, men began to develop better rockets. In the early 1800's a man in Paris named Claude Ruggieri developed small rockets which carried rats and mice into the air. The rockets were equipped with tiny automatic parachutes so that his little passengers could return to Earth safely.

Also in the early 1800's, effective rockets for war were being developed by William Congreve. They were an important weapon for England in the Napoleonic Wars with France and in the War of 1812 against the United States.

It was not until the 1920's, however, that the first real step toward modern rocketry was made. Dr. Robert H. Goddard, an American scientist, developed in 1926 the first rocket which was propelled by a liquid fuel. Before then all rockets had used a solid fuel like gunpowder. Today, most of our powerful rockets use liquid fuels such as liquid hydrogen or oxygen.

Doctor Goddard's work was not easy. It took many years of study, experiments, and tests. Some people laughed at him, others said he was a fake. After one especially noisy test-firing at a farm in Auburn, Massachusetts, many of his neighbors called the police. They thought a plane was on fire and had crashed nearby. Dr. Goddard was called before the state fire marshal. He was asked to discontinue rocket tests in the state. So, Dr. Goddard continued his experiments elsewhere. He finally developed rockets that could soar thousands of feet into the air at speeds over 600 miles an hour.

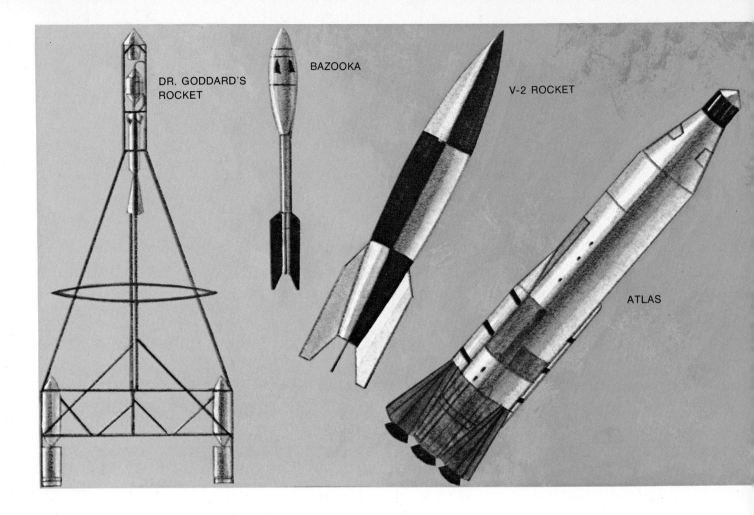

DR. GODDARD'S ROCKET

BAZOOKA

V-2 ROCKET

ATLAS

More advances in rockets came during World War II. The bazooka became an important weapon. With it, foot soldiers could launch a rocket powerful enough to destroy a tank. The Russians used larger rockets fired from launching pads on the ground or from trucks. These rockets helped the Russians defeat the Germans in the fierce battles of Stalingrad and Leningrad.

In Germany, scientists developed the V-2 rocket. This giant rocket could travel over 200 miles. It could travel at 3,000 miles an hour, which was a fantastic rate of speed for the 1940's. The V-2's brought terror and destruction to London during World War II.

In the short period from the end of World War II in 1945 to the 1960's, men made giant strides in the devel-

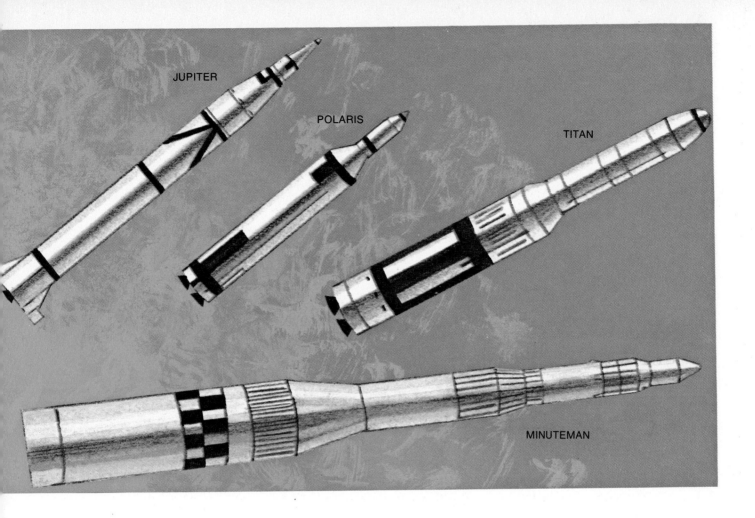

opment of rockets and missiles. In less than 20 years, rocket scientists advanced from the V-2 rocket which could travel 200 miles to rockets which could soar out past many of the planets.

Missiles became an important part of the U.S. national defense system. A *missile* is the name we give to an armed rocket—one that carries a warhead or bomb. Today, there are intercontinental ballistic missiles (ICBM's) that can carry a powerful warhead halfway around the world and deliver it exactly on target.

But more in line with the hopes and dreams of Doctor Goddard are the incredibly complex and powerful rockets that took us to the moon. Perhaps one day even greater rockets will take us to other solar systems.

How Rockets and Missiles Fly

3 . . . 2 . . . 1 . . . *FIRE!* Then a tremendous roar. For a split-second the rocket seems to hesitate. A great sheet of flame rushes from the tail, and the rocket pushes away from its launch pad. It moves at first as if in slow motion, struggling against the pull of Earth's gravity. It surges upward, gaining speed, a trail of hot flames streaking behind. Soon it is only a speck in the sky, and then it has disappeared from sight.

Rockets and missiles can go farther and much faster than any other form of transportation on Earth. Yet, like a car or a motorboat or an airplane, they are powered

by an engine. Fuel is fed into the engine and burned. The burning of fuel in the engine makes energy. This energy is the power which moves the vehicle.

Rockets have either a *liquid fuel* engine or a *solid fuel* engine. In both types of engines, the fuel is a combination of chemicals.

In a liquid fuel engine, the fuel is combined with an *oxidizer* (a chemical which adds oxygen to the fuel). Both the fuel and the oxidizer are carried in separate tanks or compartments in the rocket. Through tubes, they are pumped into a *combustion chamber*. There the fuel burns fiercely. As it burns, hot gases rush out the rear of the rocket through what is called a *thrust chamber*.

The hot gases rushing out of the rear of the rocket create a strong force. The blast of the hot gases in one direction creates a force pushing in the opposite direction. This is what causes the rocket to move forward. It is a *counterforce*, which we call *thrust*.

The more powerful the force of hot gases rushing out the rear of a rocket, the more powerful the thrust will be. Larger rockets need a very powerful thrust to be able to lift their heavy cargo and surge away from the Earth's gravity.

A solid fuel rocket, like a liquid fuel rocket, also uses a combination of chemicals. The chemicals, however, are mixed before they are loaded onto the rocket. A fuel is combined with an oxidizer and certain other chemicals. A mixer churns them together. After the mixing, the fuel is a gooey, syrup-like mass. It is poured into the rocket's engine case and allowed to "age" for several days. It slowly becomes a rubbery substance, called a *solid fuel*.

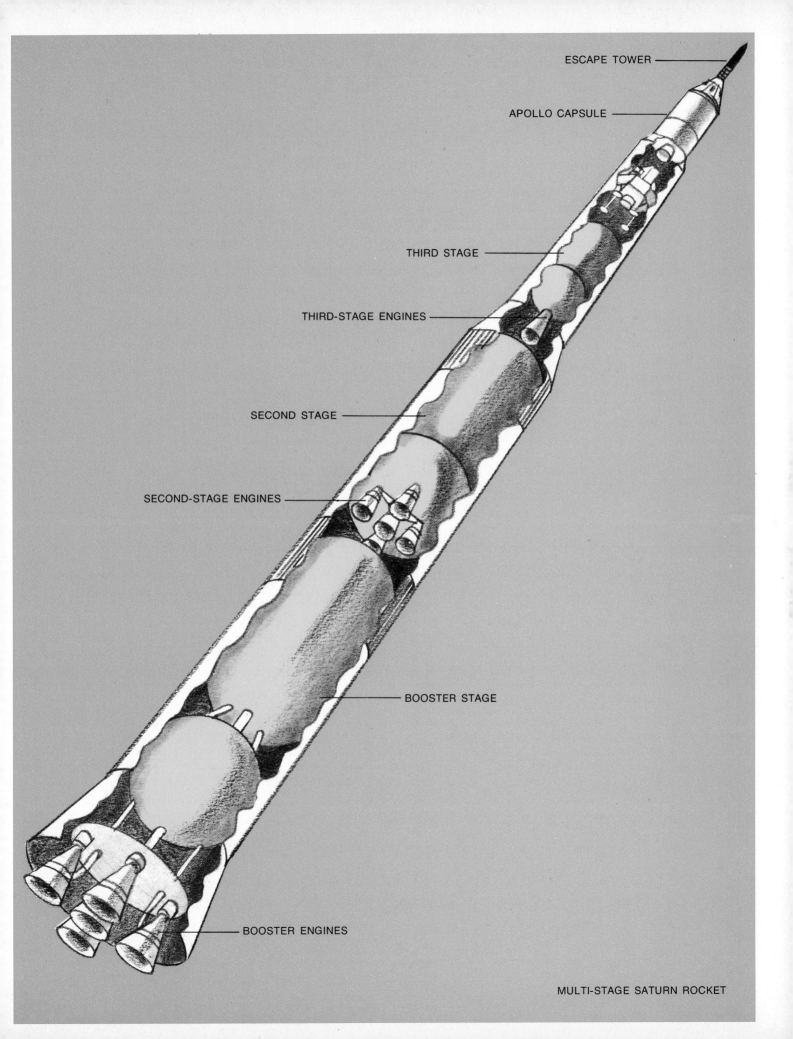

ESCAPE TOWER

APOLLO CAPSULE

THIRD STAGE

THIRD-STAGE ENGINES

SECOND STAGE

SECOND-STAGE ENGINES

BOOSTER STAGE

BOOSTER ENGINES

MULTI-STAGE SATURN ROCKET

Solid fuels cannot be regulated like liquid fuels. The flow of liquid fuels can be controlled. But a solid fuel burns steadily until it has burned itself out.

Some day scientists will develop atomic engines which will use nuclear power. A tremendous amount of energy can be produced from a very small amount of fuel in an atomic engine. This, of course, will be a great help for distant journeys deep into outer space.

Multi-stage rockets are used for extra power and speed. All of the rockets which are used for space exploration are multi-stage rockets. The first stage of a multi-stage rocket is released when it burns out. The next stage gives the rocket additional thrust. If a rocket is traveling 10,000 miles per hour when the first stage burns out, and the thrust produced by the second stage is also equal to 10,000 miles per hour, the rocket's speed will go up to 20,000 miles per hour.

Flights into outer space require a great deal of team-work. Scientists and engineers must develop the engines and guidance systems. Maintenance people check and recheck the operation of even the smallest instrument. Astronauts must be trained. But the work is going on, and man is making giant strides in exploring outer space.

Satellites
and Space Exploration

THE GREAT AGE of space exploration has begun. Travel in outer space is no longer a dream. Man has landed on the moon. Space vehicles have safely landed on the planet Venus. Space probes have sent back to Earth highly detailed photographs of the planet Mars.

Great advances have been made since the day in 1957 when the Russians successfully launched the first man-made satellite into orbit around the Earth. It was on October 4, 1957, that *Sputnik I*, a 184-pound sphere, was sent up. Four months later, on January 31, 1958, the United States launched *Explorer I*.

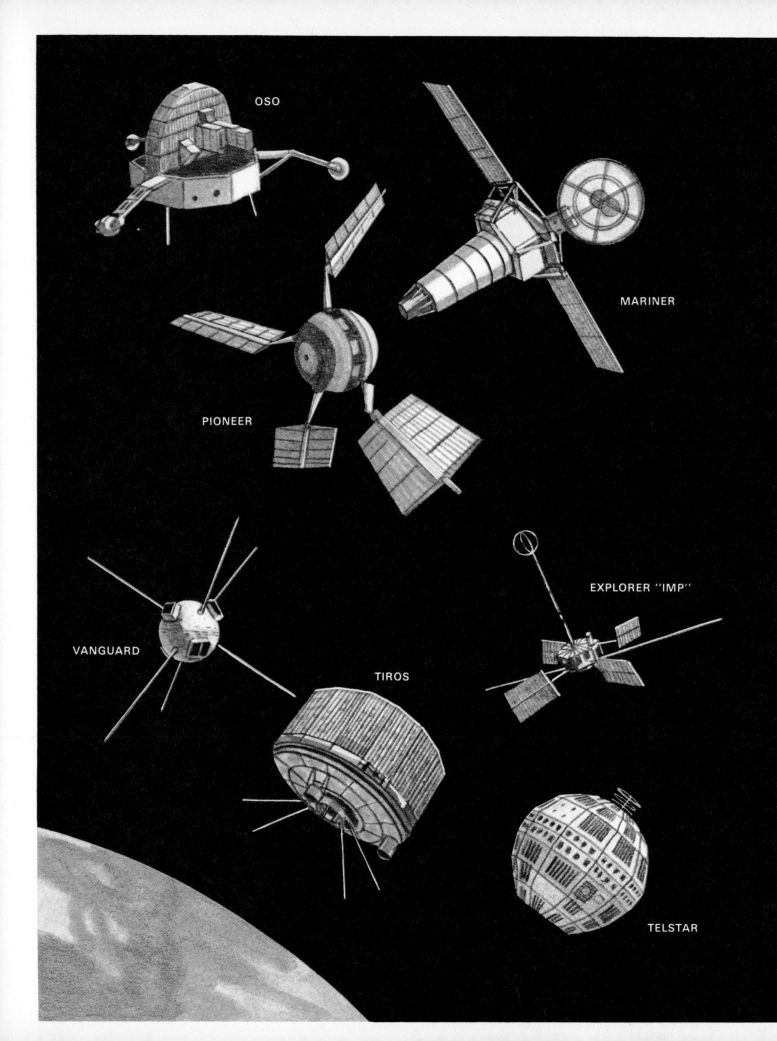

Now there are many different types of space vehicles. All, of course, are powered by rockets. A *satellite* is simply an object which orbits around a planet or sun. Our moon, in fact, is called a satellite. There are also *space probes*. A space probe soars out into space toward the moon, other planets or the sun. *Mariner IX,* a space probe launched by the United States, soared toward Mars. Somewhere in space, probes usually go into orbit. Mariner IX went into orbit around Mars and became its satellite.

Each space vehicle has a definite purpose. A satellite carrying astronauts into space may be testing the extreme conditions that man will face in space travel. Scientists study the effects of the tremendous pressure on man as the powerful rocket ship blasts off. We experience a little of this pressure when an automobile starts quickly and we are pressed back against the seat. Scientists also need to know how a man will react to the fantastic speeds at which rockets travel. And, of course, there is *weight-lessness* — man floats like a balloon in space because there is no gravity. These and many other things must be studied before space travel for us is possible.

Unmanned satellites serve many different functions. Weather or *meteorological* satellites take photographs of cloud formations and measure frontal movements.

Other unmanned satellites receive radio and television signals from Earth and transmit them back. These are *communications* satellites. They are like a giant transmitting tower 200 miles high. They can receive the television signals of a parade in Moscow and relay them back to us in the United States. This allows us to watch the parade on television as it is actually happening.

Astronomical satellites are giant telescopes in space which can observe and photograph the other heavenly bodies far better than any telescopes on Earth. Other satellites photograph the physical characteristics of the Earth.

Space probes, on the other hand, often investigate conditions far out in space. They take photographs and measure conditions of other planets. This information, which we could not ordinarily find out from Earth, is then sent back to us. *Venus VI,* a space probe launched by Russia, parachuted an instrumented capsule to a soft-landing on Venus. We had thought the temperature on Venus was similar to ours on Earth. *Venus VI* found it to be about 800 degrees. Earlier Venus probes measured the atmosphere on Venus and found very little oxygen. Because of this, it was concluded that no life like that found on Earth could survive on Venus. Space probes are actually the forerunners of the space vehicles that will take men to other planets.

Neighbors in Space

YEARS AGO, PEOPLE WROTE stories about space travel, but few of them really believed the idea. Most of these stories were about life on Venus or Mars. These planets are our closest neighbors. It was easiest for people to imagine that there was life on the planets nearest the Earth.

Then astronomers began to find out just how big the universe really is. Many people think of outer space as just a dark bowl-shaped sky full of cold glittering stars. Actually the stars are far from cold. They are glowing balls of heat, just like our sun.

Soon scientists began to think that *many* stars must have planets around them. Let's take just our own corner of the universe—our *galaxy*. The Milky Way Galaxy has billions and billions of stars (or suns) in it. Some scientists think that as many as 50 billion of these stars may have planets circling around them. Some of these stars may have just two or three planets, or nine planets like our solar system, or perhaps even hundreds of planets.

Of course, all the possible solar systems are not in our galaxy. There are millions of other galaxies throughout the universe. Each of these galaxies has billions of stars, too. Scientists know very little about the stars in other galaxies because they are so far away. But they think that many of those stars are suns, too, and probably have planets revolving around them.

This is why many scientists today think that there must be life somewhere else—because there are so many "somewhere elses." It would be *harder* to believe that the earth is the only place where there are living things.

If there *are* living things somewhere else in the universe, where are they? And what are they like?

These are the two big questions that no one can answer yet. Writers and TV programs have shown "creatures from outer space" with twelve arms or striped tentacles or antennae on their heads. Such things *could* be true, because twelve arms or green skin or three eyes might be very handy for living on certain kinds of planets!

On earth, plants and animals need oxygen and water and sunlight to stay alive. On some other planet, circling around some other sun, creatures might need very

different things to stay alive. Scientists do not expect to find another world exactly like ours.

Our Earth itself has changed greatly over millions and billions of years. During all those years, there have been many kinds of living things here.

This is another thing to remember in thinking about living things on other worlds. We might find another planet where there might be tiny plants or animals that we could see only through a microscope. Or we might find a planet where all living things lived in the sea. Or one where the only living things were plants, not animals. Or there might be kinds of life that we cannot imagine or ever understand fully.

Any of these kinds of outer space life are possible, of course. But they are not what we hope to find. We like to think that someday we will find another planet where there is *intelligent* life. We hope to find living creatures who would be able to think and talk or communicate with us in some way. They might even be much more advanced than people on earth are.

These *intelligent* outer space creatures will have to be able to do certain things—or we will never be able to meet them. They have to be able to think about things and build things. They will be able to move around. Maybe they will fly above the surface of their planet, or move on little wheels, or run on sixteen legs! But they will have to move and to have something they can use the way we use our hands.

Any creature that will communicate across space will have to be able to build very complicated machines. And even a very smart tree couldn't do that because it has

no "hands." Probably fish or water creatures couldn't build machines either.

So the "friends" we may find on another planet will be like us in that way, at least. They will also have to have something like our eyes and ears and fingers, to help them sense and understand the things around them. But on planets with strange and different things to see and hear and touch, these senses could be very different.

Right now, we "Earthlings" still do not have a good way to talk to anybody on another planet. Our radio beams are not strong enough to travel across billions of miles of space. Our spaceships and rockets cannot travel fast enough to reach another star.

90

Probably our first way of contacting space neighbors
will be radio. Scientists are working hard on building
better radio equipment. Even when we can make a very
strong radio beam, though, we will not know in what
direction to send our messages. We still do not know
where in the galaxy or the universe there may be someone to receive the message. So we are also working to
build huge radio *receivers*. These are great bowls that
can pick up very faint, faraway radio signals.

From where? From whom?

From those intelligent outer space creatures that we
think might be somewhere in our galaxy or in our
universe. If we are curious about them, chances are that

they are just as curious about us! They can do all the things we talked about—move around, sense things, build things, think about things.

To do all these things takes *curiosity*. And, just like us, these intelligent, curious creatures would probably begin to wonder if they were all alone in the universe. These faraway neighbors may be more advanced than we are. Perhaps their telescopes and radio beams are strong enough to reach across billions of miles of space.

Many scientists think that other planets may be trying to reach us in other ways. So they have built huge radio-telescopes that listen for messages from outer space—just a few *blips* or *bleeps* arranged in a special pattern that could not be an accident.

Perhaps, on some planet circling a faraway star, someone has looked through a powerful telescope. This creature has seen another bright star with nine small planets spinning around it. The first one is tiny and very close to the sun-star. The second is covered with thick clouds. But the third planet is blue, with a thin circle of atmosphere around it.

So someone—or something—on that far planet pushes a button. The first message starts across billions of space-miles, to let listeners on earth know that we do have neighbors in the universe!

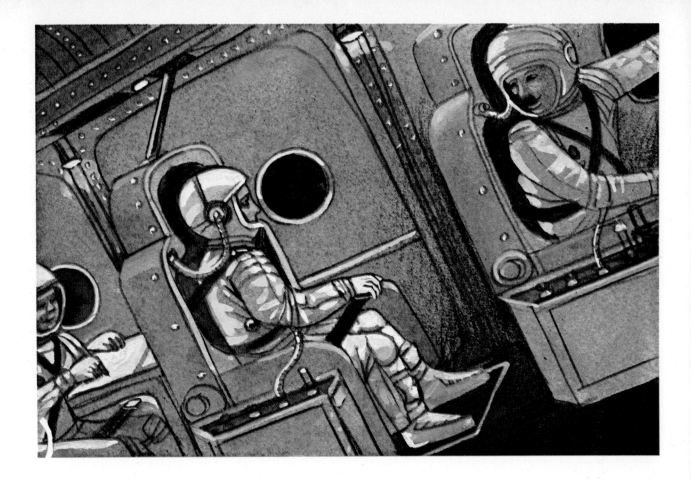

Will You Travel in Space?

TRAVEL IN OUTER SPACE is going to be quite different from any form of travel we have on Earth.

You will wear a special outfit—a pressure suit. This is to help your body withstand the tremendous pressures of take-off and re-entry. There are also strong pressures when the spacecraft accelerates and decelerates (speeds up and slows down). The pressure suit will also keep your body at a comfortable, steady temperature. Temperatures in outer space may vary from boiling hot to freezing cold, and they may change very suddenly, even when you aren't expecting it.

You will probably board a powerful but short-range rocket. The rocket will have to be powerful enough to surge away from the Earth's gravity. But it will be small because it will only be making a short trip of perhaps a few thousand miles, like the *Columbia,* the space shuttle launched successfully by the United States in 1981. The sliding doors will be sealed to maintain the pressurized cabin. You will be securely strapped into a seat.

The tremendous pressure of the blast-off pins you to the back of your seat. The rocket surges away from Earth. It reaches a speed in orbit of somewhere around 18,000 miles an hour, very slow for travel in outer space. Your destination is a large space station orbiting Earth that was put there earlier.

As you speed toward a rendezvous with the space station that is your destination, you see the great curve of Earth from your cabin window. Earth looks like a greenish-blue ball, and you can see outlines of continents and oceans.

The rocket maneuvers in and docks at the space station. There you leave the craft and board another rocket ship. The size of this spacecraft depends on where you are headed for. If you are going to the moon, it will probably be a small spaceship. If you are going to a planet, it will be a much larger spaceship.

The blast-off from the space station would not really be a blast-off at all. There would be no gravity to fight against, and the spacecraft would streak off into space. It may reach speeds of hundreds of thousands of miles an hour. However, you will not feel the speed. The only sense of movement you will have is when the rocket ship speeds up or slows down. When the speed is constant or steady, it will be as if you were standing still.

The powerful engines of the rocket will not be heard. Inside the cabin the only noises will be from instruments and equipment inside the spacecraft.

Travel in a spacecraft will present special problems. You will be weightless. When you unstrap yourself from the seat, you could float through the cabin like a feather. Therefore, you will be wearing special shoes. The soles of the shoes may be coated with an adhesive so they stick to the floor. You will be able to walk but it will be like walking across flypaper—one foot lifted at a time.

Dinner will not be served by a smiling stewardess, who places a tray in front of you. If she did, it would float right off the tray. You would even have to chase your water around the cabin. Instead you will eat preprocessed foods from something like a toothpaste tube, and you will drink only through a straw.

You will have to be very careful as you move about the cabin. If you turned a door handle, you might very well turn a complete cartwheel. Trying to turn a bolt with a wrench might result in your doing a somersault. There is no gravity to keep you down, and when you exert a force one way, the opposite force could flip you completely over.

When you reach the moon or another planet, you will probably have to change spaceships again at another space station. Or perhaps the capsule in which you are riding will detach itself from the body of the rocket ship. The rocket ship will stay in orbit and only the capsule will take you to your destination.

But you will be on your way—traveling in outer space. It will be an exciting trip, and you may very well be taking it some day.

Numbers and

Discoveries

Early Ways of Counting

COUNTING IS EASY for us today. But it took a long time for man to work out our counting system. For many thousands of years no one could count. There was not much need for counting in primitive days, because people worried most about finding food and a place to sleep. They did not own anything they had to count.

No one knows just how or why people began to count. It may be that parents needed a way to make sure none of their children were lost. Counting may also have helped men and women keep track of their animals and their other possessions. The fact is that people did begin

to count and soon invented numbers. Without numbers, the world we live in now would not be the same.

Man probably first began to count on his fingers. Later, perhaps, he put down one pebble for one animal or one club, two pebbles for two animals or two clubs. One day he wanted to tell his neighbors how many animals or clubs he owned. It would take too long to count out pebbles again and again, so he invented special noises (which we now call "words") to stand for ⬭⬭⬭⬭⬭ or ⬭⬭⬭⬭ or ⬭⬭⬭⬭⬭⬭⬭ . In this way a word came to stand for a collection of pebbles.

At first, only a few number names were invented. Even today some primitive tribes do not have any names for a number larger than five. One tribe of hunters in Australia counts things in groups of two. The word for *one* is "enea" and the word for *two* is "petcheval." When they want to say *three,* they say "petcheval-enea." *Four* is "petcheval-petcheval" and *five* is "petcheval-petcheval-enea." It must take them a long time to say 101!

When men began to barter and trade, they needed to keep records. They then had to find a way of writing down numbers. The earliest written numbers we know of were used in Egypt and Mesopotamia 5,000 years ago. These first "numbers" were notches cut in wood or stone. Later the Egyptians kept records on papyrus, a kind of paper which was made from reeds. The Mesopotamians used a wedge-shaped stick called a stylus to make dents on soft clay tablets which they baked in the sun. In that way their documents became almost as permanent as stone.

The Egyptians used straight lines, or strokes, to indicate numbers up to 9. When they reached 10, they made a picture that looked like a heel mark. When they reached 100, they drew a picture of a coiled rope. One thousand was shown by a lotus flower, 10,000 by a bent finger, and 100,000 by a fish. They built up any number they wanted by repeating strokes and marks as necessary.

GREEK

HINDU-ARABIC

ROMAN

The Greeks used letters of their alphabet to represent numbers. The "A" in their alphabet represented *one,* the "B" stood for *two* and so forth. They also used the Egyptian idea of repeating single strokes. The ancient Hebrews used their alphabet in the same way.

Probably you have seen the numbers used by the Romans. Roman numerals are still often used to mark book chapters, the faces of clocks, and building cornerstones. These numerals probably were straight lines at first. These were easy to understand because they were so little changed from the earlier finger counting. They look like letters, but they began as pictures. The numeral for five represented a hand with five fingers. Eventually the middle fingers were omitted, and the numeral became a V. Six was the five fingers of one hand plus one on the other hand, or VI. Seven was five plus two or VII.

Ten was two V's placed one atop another to form an X. These numerals were repeated to stand for larger numbers. The Roman numeral XXXII meant three tens and two ones, or 32. Fifty was represented by an L. Two L's were joined together like the V's to form a C, representing 100. D meant 500 and M stood for 1,000. Roman numerals were used in Europe for many centuries, but they were very awkward for adding, subtracting, multiplying, and dividing.

The numerals we use today are called "Arabic," because we got them from the Arabs. The Arabs, however, got them from the Hindus. Therefore, mathematicians usually give credit to both, and call them "Hindu-Arabic numerals."

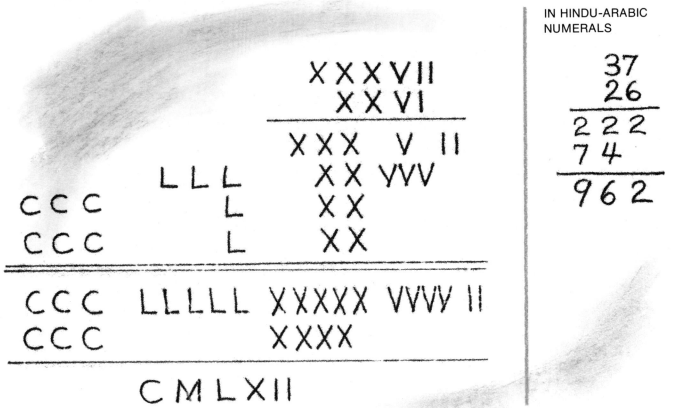

IN ROMAN NUMERALS

Whatever we call it, our system of numerals is a good one because it is more useful and easier to use than Roman numerals. It makes us think that the Hindus and Arabs must have done more with mathematics than just count sheep. They must have used their numeral systems often.

We need only ten different symbols in Hindu-Arabic: 0,1,2,3,4,5,6,7,8, and 9. We can write unlimited numbers with these symbols because each symbol can have a different meaning. Each of the first 10 numbers has a name. Then they are repeated. *Twenty* comes from an ancient word that meant "two tens." *Thirteen* comes from an old word that meant "three more than ten." Ten tens are a *hundred,* a word so old we do not know where it came from. Then we start over with one hundred plus one and go up to 200. By the time we get to 10 hundred, we use a new word, *thousand.* But we can still write all these quantities with our first ten symbols.

Scientists who work with big quantities use *kilo* to mean a thousand and *mega* to mean a million. They also use a shorthand in dealing with large numbers. It would take too much time and space to write out 10,000,000,000,000,000,000 (10 billion billion). Instead, the number of zeroes is written as a small "exponent" to the upper right of the 10, like this: 10^{19}. One hundred has two zeroes and is written 10^2. A thousand is 10^3.

It is quite difficult to get along in our civilization today with just simple arithmetic. We are surrounded with figures. We need more math to solve our everyday problems. We need several different kinds of mathematics. We need advanced mathematics to study astronomy or economics. We learn short cuts in studying *algebra.* *Geometry* is the study of shapes and sizes of things and how much you can put in them. *Trigonometry* uses information learned in algebra as a tool for measuring distances, such as the distance from the earth to the moon. *Calculus* is used to solve problems about things that are always changing, like the speed of a bomb dropping out of an airplane.

Mathematics is the tool used by all sciences to solve problems—and so it is sometimes called the queen of the sciences.

The World of Computers

COMING BACK TO EARTH safely is one of the trickiest parts of a space flight. Whenever astronauts are ready to return after successfully orbiting the earth, there has to be careful, split-second planning in order to bring the capsule down safely.

First, the space pilots must know exactly when to fire their retro-rockets. The scientists who plan the flight must figure out how many seconds these rockets must burn so that the spaceship will land in the ocean near rescue ships. Working with paper and pencil, it would take scientists years to do the necessary arithmetic. The

space capsule might have to orbit for many years waiting for the arithmetic to be done!

However, space scientists have a very special machine to do this work. The electronic computer does millions of problems in addition, subtraction, multiplication, and division in only a second, and tells scientists exactly when the rockets should be fired.

The computer is one of the most remarkable inventions of this century. It is changing the lives of everyone, just as television, radio, the automobile, and the jet engine have made our lives very different from the lives of our grandfathers.

Computers do the same thing that people do when they count, only they do it with incredible speed. Computers also "remember." When we multiply or divide, we keep certain numbers in our head to "carry over." If there are too many numbers, we tend to forget. The

computer can keep millions of numbers in its "brain," and recall them instantly. It remembers, for example, where all of a railroad company's 125,000 freight cars are from minute to minute. It remembers the number of seats in all the airplanes of an airline, and can tell at once whether there is a seat available for a passenger in Detroit who wants to go to Los Angeles at 6:05 on Tuesday. Unlike human beings, the computer never gets tired, never gets bored, and never forgets.

In olden days, people kept track of things by piling up sticks or stones or by making marks in the sand or on cave walls. The ancient Chinese developed the *abacus,* which is a frame with beads strung on wires. Each bead represents a number. Today's desk-top adding machine is modeled after the abacus.

The first true electronic computer was invented in 1944. It was used during World War II to compute where ships should fire their torpedoes. It weighed 30

tons and filled an entire room. Now computers are built as small as a hatbox and can be carried in a space capsule. Computers of the future will be made even smaller.

The computer that counts is called a *digital computer*. There is another type that measures. It is called an *analog computer*. The speedometer in an automobile is a kind of analog computer. The odometer, the dial that counts the miles traveled, is an example of a digital computer.

Today's computers are used to prepare payrolls for big businesses, to design ships, airplanes, roadways and bridges, to forecast weather, to solve building problems, and even to catch criminals.

Tomorrow's computers will do even more. They will memorize and store up every page of every book in huge libraries. Home computers may become very helpful members of the family. Punching the keys of the home computer will bring to every schoolchild the library information he needs to do his homework. The same computer will send orders to grocery stores and let

people vote without leaving the house. It will keep the household budget, plan menus, figure income tax, and remind us of appointments. It will even shut the windows when it rains.

You will be able someday to push a button and fill your living room with musical scores never heard before. Your "composer-computer" will be told what you like and dislike in music, and it will select a number of pleasing sound combinations from an electronic sound-wave maker.

Computers will help doctors by making measurements of the heart, brain, liver, and other organs. They will help the doctor find out what is wrong with people, and tell him what treatment to give them. They will let a doctor in the United States "consult" with doctors all over the world who have treated the same sickness. If a doctor needs to transplant a heart or a kidney to a sick patient, he will be able to find out from a computer network where he can get the spare part.

Computers that read aloud from printed texts will one day "read" books for blind people. Computers also will be able to read handwriting and to translate foreign languages. They will be able to listen to voices and reply.

Sometimes the computer's skills start us wondering whether it will replace people. But no machine has ever been built that can do what the human brain can do. If there were one, it would have to be as tall as a skyscraper, and it would need all the electrical power of Niagara Falls to run it. A computer may be fast, but it still cannot think for itself. It must be told what to do.

As with all the machines man has invented to save himself time and trouble, the computer will free people from long and boring work. In many countries, all members of the family must devote all their waking hours to finding and preparing food. They have no time to relax. Computers will provide us more leisure and they will also give us time and the ability to go on learning more and more—about how things work, about new ideas and information. In these ways, computers will make our lives better.

Alchemists Search
for Gold

ABOUT 2,000 YEARS AGO there arose a cult of people known as *alchemists*. They are called a cult because their work was secret. They believed they could find a magic formula that would turn cheap metals, like tin and lead, into glittering gold.

Alchemists worked in smoky, smelly laboratories. Into their boiling pots they tossed such things as herbs, flowers, blood, horseradish, ashes, bat's wings, and a few drops of strong acid. Kings and emperors, hoping to get rich, made alchemists special members of their court. The alchemists were given many special privileges.

But alchemy was not altogether a safe occupation. When an alchemist failed to produce gold, the king might order him put to death. Therefore, some alchemists turned to trickery. They gave common metal a yellowish color and passed it off as gold.

The final blow to alchemy came when a British alchemist presented a sample of "gold" to King George III. However, some scientists doubted that he had made gold, and they demanded that he do it in front of them. The alchemist tried to escape the test, but was forced by the king to agree. On the day of the test he walked to the center of the room, lifted a flask to his lips and drank. He fell dead in a few seconds. The flask contained poison.

Trickery gave the alchemists a bad reputation, but their work was not all bad. They helped lay the groundwork for modern chemistry. They introduced several acids used in chemistry now. They also designed stills, retorts, crucibles, and other tools still used in today's laboratories.

There was one other false belief from the days of alchemy that had to be proved wrong before modern chemistry came into being. This was the belief about *phlogiston*. Even real men of science, not just alchemists, believed that anything that burned had this strange "substance," phlogiston, in it. When wood burned, they thought, phlogiston escaped as flame.

Robert Boyle, who lived 300 years ago, did not believe this. He insisted there was something in the air that made things burn. To prove his point, he put a lighted candle under a glass jar and then gradually removed the air. The candle flame died out. He did the experiment again with a live mouse and a lighted candle under the jar. The mouse died and the candle went out about the same time.

Some time later it was discovered that it was *oxygen* in the air that made things burn. Oxygen is needed not only for the kind of fires that produce flames, but also for the "chemical fire" in our bodies that turns the food we eat into energy. The discovery of oxygen, followed by the discovery of *atoms*, opened the door to modern chemistry.

In about 1803, John Dalton, a Quaker schoolmaster, first explained how atoms work. He said that all the chemical elements that make up our world and our universe are composed of *atoms.* He said, too, that an atom of one element can join with one or more atoms of another element to form a *molecule.* For example, one atom of the element sodium combines with one atom of the element chlorine to form a molecule of table salt. To anyone who has studied chemistry, "Please pass the sodium chloride" is just the same as "Please pass the salt."

Two atoms of the element hydrogen combine with one atom of the element oxygen to form a molecule of water. If you ever hear water called "H_2O," that is what it means—two hydrogen atoms (H_2) and one oxygen (O).

There are millions of molecules in a teaspoonful of drinking water. If each one of these tiny water molecules could be enlarged to the size of a raindrop, that teaspoonful of water would then fill Lake Michigan.

What the ancient alchemist could never do, the modern physicist can do. It is possible today to turn lead into gold by using a *cyclotron,* or "atom smasher." But the cost of doing so is far greater than the value of the gold produced. It is still true for us, as it was for the alchemist, that there is no magic way to wealth.

The World of Chemistry

WE ROLL SLEEPILY OUT of bed in the morning and immediately enter into the world of modern chemistry. We slip on a chemical (nylon) robe and walk to the bathroom on a chemical (rayon) rug. We reach for a toothbrush whose handle is plastic, made by chemistry, and whose bristles are another kind of plastic. Chemicals called fluorides have been added to the toothpaste we use to help protect teeth against decay. Soap is a chemical creation, and so is its pleasant smell.

At the breakfast table, the foods are plentiful because chemical fertilizers have enriched the soil in which the corn, wheat, and oats in our bread and cereals grow. The morning paper that your father is reading is printed on paper made from wood pulp by a chemical process. If we climb into an automobile or bus to go to work or to school, we are riding in a chemical vehicle. From the safety glass windshield in front to the steel bumpers in the rear, chemistry has built much of the modern car.

Even the power that moves the car or bus comes from chemistry. All gasoline is chemically processed from crude oil taken from the ground. From the same dark and sticky oil, chemists also get airplane fuel and the heavy oil to run the diesel engines of the big railroad locomotives and trucks.

Today's automobile also runs on "chemical" tires which were developed by chemists in World War II. Supplies of natural rubber from southeast Asia were cut off then, and chemists were asked to find a substitute. They showed that artificial rubber could be made better and cheaper in the laboratory than nature makes it.

The chemists' dream of making a fiber from hydrogen, carbon, and oxygen, all ordinary chemicals, was fulfilled about 50 years ago when they made nylon from coal, natural gas, petroleum, air, and water. Nylon made beautiful stockings that were stronger and longer-lasting than the natural silk stockings women used to wear. Later, shirts and dresses were made of nylon; so were fishing tackle, brushes, and hundreds of other things.

The wonder metal, aluminum, was created by a 22-year-old chemist who found a way to dissolve it out of its raw material. It is very strong and yet very much lighter than steel. Its color is silver-white. It has an attractive shine and it does not rust. We use aluminum in building tall structures, airplanes, toys, railroad cars, and electric cables. Most of the pots and pans in the kitchen are made of aluminum.

Chemistry has helped provide better nourishment for millions of people by fertilizing food plants and destroying insects and diseases that kill plants. With chemical weedkillers, fertilizers, and insecticides, a farmer can grow ten times more food today with less work than was needed a few years ago.

Chemistry also has given us drugs to kill germs that cause diseases in the body. People are living longer and healthier lives because of medicines like penicillin and streptomycin, which have come to be called "miracle" drugs. Chemistry has developed drugs that help people with mental illness and such diseases as cancer.

Without chemistry there would be no vaccine against crippling polio or typhoid fever. There would be no pain-relieving anesthetics to put us to sleep when we have an operation, and no chlorination to kill disease germs in drinking water.

When he was 84 years old and near the end of his career, the famous electrical inventor, Thomas Edison, was asked, "If you were younger, and had your life to live over again, what would you choose for your work?" Without a moment of hesitation, he said, "Chemistry. The future chemical discoveries will benefit mankind in a way we can't even dream of today."

Archimedes' Bathtub

IF YOU COULD BE WEIGHED while floating in water, you would be much lighter than you are when you stand on a scale on land. The reason is that your body is lifted, or *buoyed up,* by water. You can feel the lifting power of water if you try to lift a rock out of a lake or river. The rock feels light when it is under water, for the water is helping you lift it. When it is lifted out of the water, the rock seems much heavier.

The buoyancy (or lifting power) of liquids was first explained by a Greek philosopher and mathematician named Archimedes, who lived about 2,200 years ago.

Archimedes discovered facts about buoyancy in a most unusual way.

The story is told that Hiero, king of the Greek city of Syracuse, gave a goldsmith a lump of gold and told him to make a royal crown. The crown was delivered, and it weighed the same as the original lump of gold. But the king suspected that the goldsmith was dishonest. Perhaps he had kept some of the gold and mixed silver

with the rest of it, to make the crown heavy. Hiero called in Archimedes and asked him to find out the truth without melting down the crown.

The problem was a difficult one, and Archimedes wondered how to solve it. The answer suddenly came to him one day as he lowered himself into one of the public baths in the city. He noticed that some water overflowed over the sides of the tub. Archimedes became so excited, the story says, that he ran out of the bath house and through the streets of Syracuse, shouting, "Eureka! Eureka!" In Greek, that meant, "I have found it! I have found it!"

Archimedes made an experiment to prove the idea he had just thought of. He weighed the crown. Then he took a lump of gold and a lump of silver, each weighing the same as the crown. The lump of silver was larger because silver is lighter than gold. It takes much more of it to weigh as much as gold.

He put each of the lumps in a vessel filled to the brim with water. The larger lump of silver made more water overflow than the gold did, even though both weighed the same. Archimedes knew then that any solid material pushes away an amount of water equal to its own *volume,* or bulkiness. So if the crown were pure gold, it would have to *displace* (or push away) the same amount of water as the lump of pure gold that weighed the same.

124

But the crown made *more* water overflow than the lump of gold did. This meant the crown was not pure gold. The silver that the dishonest goldsmith had added made the crown bulkier. The goldsmith was found guilty of stealing.

Archimedes continued to experiment and found that what he had learned could be used to make a rule for things that float as well as for things that sink. Anything that floats displaces its own *weight* of water. Anything that sinks displaces an amount of water equal to its own *volume*.

Weight tells us how *heavy* something is. Volume tells how much *space* it takes up. A pound of butter and a pound of marshmallows both weigh the same—but if you pile up a pound of marshmallows, you will see that it takes up much more space, or volume.

A submarine is a good example of Archimedes' principle of buoyancy. A submarine is built so that it weighs less than the same volume of sea water does. When the captain wants to make a floating submarine submerge, he gives the order for water to be pumped into the ballast tanks. When the weight of the submarine becomes as great as the weight of the water it must push out of the way, the submarine sinks. When the captain wants to bring the submarine to the surface,

he gives the order to force the water out of the tanks. The submarine then becomes lighter than the water it displaces, and it is pushed up again.

Just like the submarine, any object will float if it weighs less than the water it displaces. It will sink if it weighs more. Sunken ships are sometimes raised by applying Archimedes' principle. Large tanks are filled with enough water to sink them. On the ocean bottom the tanks are chained to the sunken ship. Then the water in the tanks is pushed out by air that is pumped into them. If enough tanks have been used, the total buoyant force will lift the ship to the surface.

A simple experiment will prove that a floating thing displaces a weight of water equal to its own weight. First weigh a toy boat that you know will float. Next, punch a hole in a coffee can about an inch from the top. Fill the can with water up to the hole. Place the can in a large pan to catch the water, and put the toy boat in the can. Some water will flow out through the hole. Weigh this water, and you will find that it is the same as the weight of the boat.

Archimedes made another great discovery—the principle of levers. Nearly every boy has used a sturdy stick to pry up things that were too heavy for him to lift. A stick used in this way is a *lever*.

A lever makes work easier because a small force at one end can move a heavy load at the other. Archimedes said, "Give me a lever long enough and a place to stand, and I could move the earth itself." He demonstrated the power of a lever by pulling a heavily laden ship along the beach all by himself—using a lever.

The fame of Archimedes as a great inventor spread through many lands. When the king of Syracuse found his country was in danger of invasion by the Romans, he naturally called on Archimedes for help. Using levers, Archimedes built new and powerful catapults. These were weapons that worked like giant slingshots. They hurled stones weighing 500 pounds at the enemy. Archimedes also is said to have constructed a giant burning glass to focus the sun's rays on enemy ships and set them on fire.

With Archimedes' help, Syracuse staved off the Romans for several years. Eventually, however, the great city fell. There was a massacre, but the Roman commander gave orders that Archimedes was not to be harmed. Archimedes went on studying mathematics.

But one day he was sketching a diagram in the sand, as was his habit. A Roman soldier came by and ordered him to rise. Archimedes was so intent on his work that he paid no attention to the command. The soldier drew his sword and killed the greatest scientist of that time.

The Apple and Mr. Newton

"WHY DOES AN APPLE fall *down* from a tree, not up?" Isaac Newton wondered that, as he sat and looked at the apple that had almost hit him on the head.

People have told this story often to explain Newton's discovery of great truths that no one before his time had thought much about. Many people before him had seen apples and other objects fall to the ground, but no one had wondered why.

The answer that Newton found — and proved — was that there was a force called *gravity*. Earth's gravity tends to pull all objects toward the earth's center. The gravity force of the sun holds the planets in their orbits around the sun, Newton said.

Newton was a brilliant man who made many discoveries. His famous book, *Principia,* published in 1687, has been called the greatest single achievement of the human mind. When Newton died, he was buried in Westminster Abbey, an honor that England reserves for its greatest men. The words on his tomb say, "Let mortals rejoice that there has existed such and so great an ornament of the human race."

Nothing about Isaac Newton's childhood or family would have made anyone expect him to be a genius. He was a puny, sickly baby, born on Christmas day, 1642. His father died a few weeks before Newton was born. His mother was poor.

Because he was so small, Newton was unable to join in the rougher games of other boys his age. He learned to enjoy doing things by himself. He worked out games that could be played without partners. He also read a great deal. When Isaac was ten, he entered a public school and boarded with a stranger, a druggist. He was

always up to tricks that kept the poor druggist in a panic. He made little windmills that worked and kites that flew. He made clocks that ran by water power. He drew charcoal sketches on the walls of his bedroom, and he wrote poetry.

When he was 14 years old, his mother brought him home to run the family farm. But Newton was usually found studying books behind a hedge. His uncle realized Newton was no farmer, and suggested he go to college. Newton entered Trinity College, Cambridge, and soon distinguished himself in mathematics. He knew more than his professors.

A great plague raged in England in 1665, and the college was closed. Newton, now 23 years old, returned to his mother's farm. He would sit for hours in the garden thinking about the strangeness of the world. He was sitting there when the apple fell. That falling apple was one of the turning points in the history of human thought.

For nearly two years Newton thought about gravity and many other things. He would get up in the morning and, half-dressed, sit on the edge of his bed. Sometimes he would sit there and think until dinner time.

With prisms bought for a few pennies at a county fair, Newton showed that a beam of sunlight is composed of the six colors of the rainbow: red, orange, yellow, green, blue, and violet. He ground lenses and mirrors and made a new kind of microscope. He invented *calculus*, a new kind of mathematics.

He returned again and again to his ideas about gravity. The moon, he said, is caught between two forces. Gravity pulls it toward the earth. At the same time the force of its rotating, called *centrifugal force*, pulls it outward. Pulled by these two forces, the moon can neither fly toward the earth nor away from the earth. It does the next best thing—it moves in a curved path around the earth.

You can feel these two forces at work if you tie a string on a ball and whirl it in the air around you. The ball would fly away except for the string which holds it back. You can feel it pulling away. But your grip on the cord is like the force of gravity. It holds the ball so that it moves in a circle around you.

Newton then reasoned that if gravity explained the curved path of the moon, it could also explain the curved path of all the heavenly bodies. He said that just as the earth holds the moon, the sun holds the earth, the other planets, and the comets with its gravitational pull. His idea is called the Law of Universal Gravitation.

Newton's law explains why a spaceship can orbit around the earth. The whirling motion forces the capsule away from the earth, but gravity pulls the capsule toward the earth. The two forces balance one another and the spacecraft travels in an orbit.

Not many people understood Newton at first, but that is not surprising. His ideas were startlingly new and far different from what people had believed. Yet whether they always understood him or not, people recognized Newton as a man of genius.

He was elected president of the Royal Society, and held that office for 24 years. He was knighted by Queen Anne. Newton died on March 20, 1727, in his 85th year, honored as one of the greatest men ever to have lived in England.

Leeuwenhoek's "Little Beasties"

SOMETIMES CURIOSITY IS as important in science as years of studying and training. Sometimes it is *more* important. The first man to see *microbes*—tiny creatures such as bacteria—was not a scientist. He was the janitor of the town hall of Delft, in Holland. His name was Anton von Leeuwenhoek.

Leeuwenhoek left school when he was 16, and went to work in a linen shop. He learned how to use a magnifying lens to examine threads in the cloth. Eventually, he grew tired of that job and went to work in the town hall. In his spare time, though, he continued to look at

things with his magnifying glasses. He looked at a thread of wool, a drop of wine, the head of a fly, the sting of a bee, the scrapings from his own skin and teeth, the wood of different trees, and the seeds of plants.

His lenses showed details which were too small to be seen with his eyes alone. Leeuwenhoek grew more and more curious. He ground and reground the lenses to make the images even bigger and sharper. He grouped lenses together to form a simple microscope.

One day he told a fellow townsman, Regnier de Graaf, about his discoveries. De Graaf was a scientist and a corresponding member of the Royal Society of London, a famous group of scholars and scientists. De Graaf wrote a letter to the society urging them to ask Leeuwenhoek about his discoveries. Leeuwenhoek answered with a letter that was entitled, "A Specimen of Some Observations made by a Microscope contrived by Mr. Leeuwenhoek, concerning Mould Upon the Skin, Flesh, etc.; The Sting of a Bee, etc."

He wrote about 400 more long, rambling letters to the Royal Society. They were astounded by the marvelous things Leeuwenhoek told of seeing through his lenses. He had seen tiny particles in his own blood, so small that a hundred of them together were barely the size of a grain of wheat.

He clearly saw the eggs of insects in spoiled meat and cheese. Many other people of that time said that such insects were born out of nothing at all, with neither fathers nor mothers. Leeuwenhoek's discovery of the eggs of insects showed that this was impossible, and that all animals were born or hatched from other living animals.

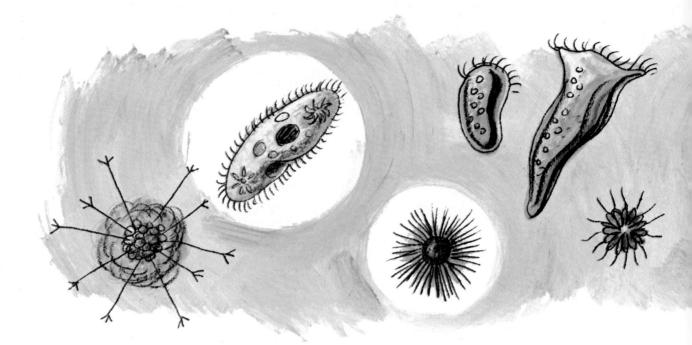

One day Leeuwenhoek put a drop of rainwater in his microscope. To his great surprise he saw "little animals" in the water. "They swim and they play around," he shouted to his daughter, Maria. "They are a thousand times smaller than any creatures we can see with our eyes alone."

Leeuwenhoek had found a fantastic tiny world of little things that lived and died completely unseen by men. They were the oldest living things on earth—yet no one had ever seen them. Leeuwenhoek wrote a letter to the Royal Society. This new discovery, though, was too startling. They could not believe he had discovered a new world of "little beasties," as he called them. So they commissioned Robert Hooke, a great British scientist, to make the best microscope he knew how and try

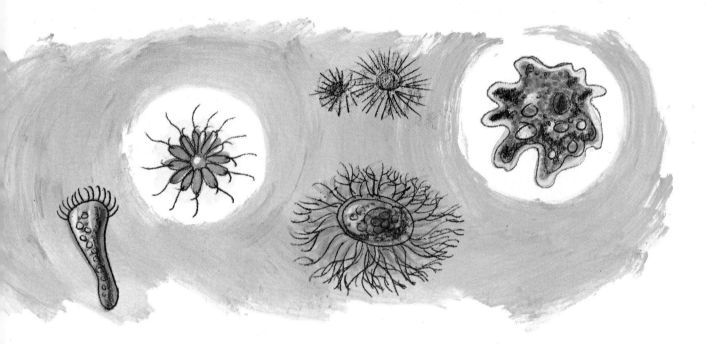

the same experiment. Hooke reported to the Royal Society that Leeuwenhoek was right. The science called *microbiology* had begun.

Where did the "beasties" in rainwater come from? Had they come down from the sky? Leeuwenhoek washed clean a big porcelain dish, walked out in the rain, caught a drop and put it before his microscope. No "little beasties" could be seen. This proved they did not come out of the sky. He put the porcelain dish aside for several days and then looked again. There they were.

Now he set to work to track down the creatures everywhere. He examined water from the roof of his house, water from the canals of Delft, water from wells and from rain barrels. He even grew his own "animals" on a few grains of pepper.

The Royal Society made him an honorary member and sent him a diploma in a silver case marked with the coat of arms of the society. It was the greatest day in the life of this humble janitor who had never been formally trained in science.

Before his death in 1723, at the age of 91, the whole of Europe had come to know Anton von Leeuwenhoek. Peter the Great, the Czar of Russia, came to pay his respects. The Queen of England traveled to Delft to look at the wonders to be seen through the lenses of his microscope.

Leeuwenhoek built almost 400 microscopes in his long lifetime. Though many people wanted them, he refused to sell any. In his will, he left the most valuable microscopes to the Royal Society.

Many scientists studied the little animals that Leeuwenhoek had brought to their attention. They named them and classified them by sizes and colors and other characteristics. Not until almost 200 years later did people realize that some bacteria produced disease in people, animals, and crops, although most of them are actually helpful to man.

Heat

ON A COLD DAY people rub their hands together to warm them. Ever since man learned to rub sticks together to start a fire, he has known he could generate heat by *friction*. Today we still start fires by friction when we strike a match. Even rubbing two ice cubes together will produce enough heat to melt them in below-freezing weather.

People long ago thought up many ways of explaining what *heat* is. But not until about 150 years ago did we understand that the secret of heat lies in tiny particles called *molecules*. Molecules are so unbelievably tiny that there are millions of them in the dot at the end of this sentence.

All molecules are constantly moving or *vibrating.* Even very solid things, like trees and buildings, are made of these fast-moving particles. Molecules in gases and liquids, though, are moving faster than those in solid substances like wood or steel. Rubbing your hands together makes the molecules in your hands vibrate faster. They bump neighboring molecules and set them into faster motion. This motion is called "heat."

When something is heated, the force that holds the molecules close to each other is loosened. The molecules are free to move about. When solid ice, for instance, is heated, it becomes water. If the water is boiled to produce steam, the molecules increase their activity still more. They swing out and fly free as *water vapor.*

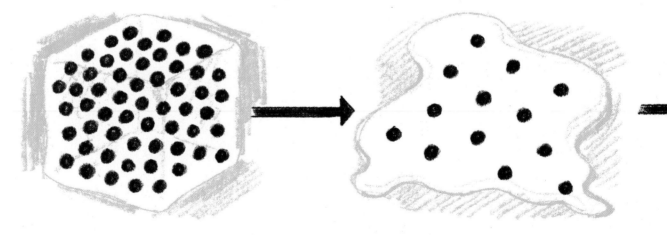

ICE

WATER

So what we call "heat" is really energy of motion of the vibrating molecules. Greatly increased energy of motion causes solids to become liquids and liquids to become gases.

This idea is called "the molecular theory of heat." It explains why the handle of a frying pan gets hot even though the handle is not over the flame. Molecules at the bottom of the pan are speeded up by the fire. They bump into their neighboring molecules and start them vibrating faster. These molecules bump into others, and so on, until eventually even the molecules in the handle are moving faster. This process of transferring heat is called *conduction*. It is very much like one bowling pin knocking down the next one, and that bowling pin hitting another, until they all fall down.

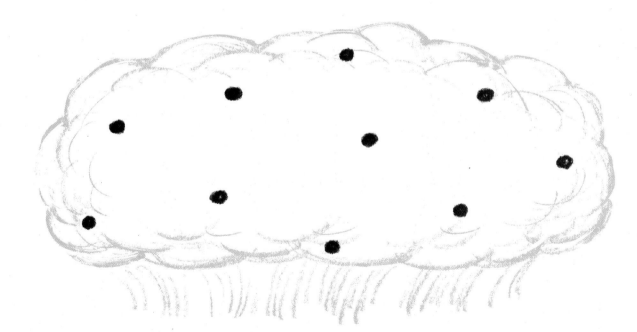

WATER VAPOR

143

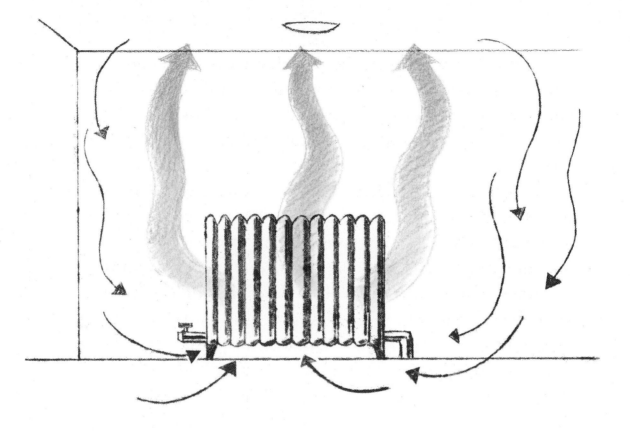

Heat also travels in other ways. Most houses are heated by *convection*. When a radiator warms a room, the air near the radiator is heated first. It expands and becomes lighter, then is pushed up by the heavier cool air around it. After giving up its heat, the air that was once warm becomes heavier and drifts downward again to pick up more heat. The rapid rise and slow settling produces a convection current that spreads heat around the room.

A furnace in a large home works in much the same way, except that the warm air is conducted by pipes to the various rooms. Cool air is carried back to the furnace by other pipes to be reheated. Some homes use hot water instead of hot air to transfer heat from the furnace to each room, through radiators or other outlets.

A third way heat can be transferred is by *radiation*. This is the process by which the sun warms the earth. The sun's heat energy is transmitted through space by waves. The earth absorbs the heat, and in turn radiates part of it.

It is lucky for us that the earth radiates some of its heat, because if it lost *no* heat, it would get hotter and hotter until no one could survive. Luckily, too, the earth does not radiate *all* of its heat. Our air, and the clouds and water vapor in the air, keep some of the heat from being lost. Fruit growers make fires to prevent their crops from freezing. It is not the warmth of the fire that helps so much as the smoke which helps shut off radiation heat loss.

WOOL FIBERS
(MAGNIFIED)

146

If the full power of the sun's heat waves came down on earth, there could be no life here. The earth would be far too hot. But once again we are protected by our air.

Air is a very poor conductor of heat. It is such a poor conductor that it is used as an insulator. A woolen blanket or sweater "warms" us because of air spaces it traps between its meshes. This air helps keep the body heat from escaping by conduction or radiation. Animals' fur also traps air and keeps them warm. Soldiers wear several layers of light clothing in the winter to take advantage of the insulating air between the layers.

Homes are built with air space between the outer and inner walls as insulation to keep in the heat during winter and to keep out cold. Storm windows and storm doors also trap insulating air. If you see a house that still has snow on the roof several weeks after a snowfall, you know that house is well insulated. It is not allowing heat to escape through the roof to melt the snow.

As scientists learn more about heat, they will probably find more exciting ways to use it. Already, scientists know how to create temperatures here on earth almost as hot as the sun. When they learn to control these very hot temperatures, scientists will have discovered a new source of energy almost as powerful as the sun itself.

Light

EARLY GREEK SCHOLARS thought the eye sent out "light-rays" to shine on an object a man wished to see. You can quickly prove this idea is not true by trying to read this book in a dark closet.

Seeing works the other way around. The object we wish to see must send out the light. You can see the page you are reading because sunlight or light from a lamp is shining on the page and bouncing into your eyes. The light enters your eye, bringing with it the image of what you are looking at. Nerves deliver a "message" about the image to your brain—and you see the page.

148

A cat's eyes appear to glow at night when a flashlight beam is shined on them. His eyes, however, are not sending out rays of light. The cat is simply reflecting the flashlight beam from a mirror-like lining at the back of his eyes.

Some things are visible because they are *luminous*; that is, they give off their own light. The sun, a fire, and an electric light bulb are examples of luminous objects. The moon is not luminous, however, even though we speak of moonlight. Moonlight is really light from the sun which is bouncing off the moon.

Things that are dark soak up most of the light that falls on them. Very little of the light bounces off, or is *reflected*. Therefore, these dark objects are harder to see. Light-colored objects, however, reflect more light. A mirror is one of the best reflectors known. It is simply a sheet of glass with a shiny, light-colored coating on the back.

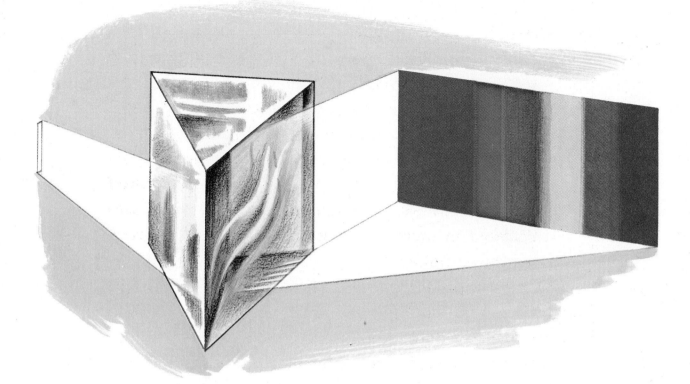

One of the most important experiments on light was made by Sir Isaac Newton, greatest of all English men of science. (See the chapter on Newton on page 129.) About 300 years ago he discovered that white light (sunshine) is made up of many colors. He passed a beam of white light through a *prism*—a triangular piece of glass—and found that the light spread out in a band of six colors: red, orange, yellow, green, blue, and violet. When he sent this light through a second prism, the light that emerged was white once more. Newton had taken white light apart and put it together again.

Probably the commonest example of a *spectrum* of color is nature's rainbow. A rainbow is caused by sunlight shining on water droplets in the air just after a summer shower. The thousands of water droplets break up the light just as a prism does. You can make your own rainbow by turning on the fine spray of a garden hose with the sunlight coming over your shoulder.

What is light, and how does it travel from place to place? At one time there were great arguments among scientists about these questions. Sir Isaac Newton believed that light was made up of tiny particles that flowed in a stream from the light source. Other scientists said light traveled in waves like the waves seen when a rock is tossed into a pond.

Now it is believed that both ideas were right. Light behaves both as a stream of particles and as waves. It does consist of tiny packets of energy called *photons*. Light also is made up of various waves, and the length of these waves determines the color of the light. Red light has about 40,000 waves to the inch, and violet has about 70,000 waves to the inch. In between are the other colors of the light spectrum.

There are "colors," however, that are invisible. Infrared has fewer waves to the inch than red light, and ultraviolet has more waves to the inch than violet. Human eyes cannot see these "colors," but special photographic films and other devices can "see" them.

WAVE LENGTHS OF LIGHT
Measured in microns. One micron equals .00004 inch.

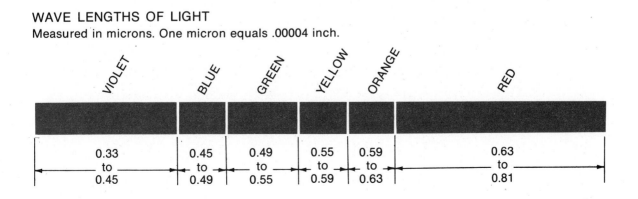

Nothing in the universe is known to travel faster than light. It can travel more than four times around the world while you are saying your name. The sunlight you see now left the sun 93 million miles away only 8½ minutes ago. Light from some of the stars has taken billions of years to get here. That will give you some idea of how incredibly far away those stars are.

Scientists have discovered an unusual device that produces a strange new kind of light. This new device is called a *laser* (sounds like "razor"). The laser produces a beam of light powerful enough to cut through metal. Doctors use lasers to perform bloodless surgery. Military men think lasers might be used as a death ray. Engineers think lasers might be used for instant welding or boring a hole in a diamond.

Instead of spreading out, as does the light in a beam from a searchlight or flashlight, the light from a laser is concentrated in a tight beam. None of the light energy is wasted.

One laser has sent its intense beam of light to the moon and back in less than three seconds. Surgeons have re-attached torn parts of the eye by welding them with a laser. They have burned away diseased cells of the body. Dentists say it might be possible to harden teeth with a laser beam so they will never decay.

The laser is a better range finder than radar. It is better at carrying radio, telephone, and TV signals than the methods we now use. In the future we shall probably use laser beams for these and other communications. One narrow laser beam can carry many TV programs or telephone conversations without the choppy interference we often get with our present system. A single laser beam could carry over 100 million telephone conversations.

Astronauts will probably use the laser to talk to Earth from deep space. Lasers also might be used as a weapon against enemy missiles.

Sound

THE WORLD IS FULL of different sounds: the buzz of a fly, the tick of a watch, the ring of a telephone, the screaming of a siren, the roar of a jet airplane. Yet all sounds are alike in one way. Every sound is caused by a rapid back-and-forth movement, or quivering, that we call *vibration*. When something vibrates, it sends sound waves into the air.

Your sense of touch will tell you that sound is connected with vibration. If you touch a radio that is playing loudly, you can feel it quivering. The strings of a guitar quiver when they make a sound.

When you speak you create vibrations in the air with your vocal cords. Fish make sounds by forcing air from their swim bladders. The hum of a mosquito is produced by the rapid movement of its wings, more than 100 times a second.

When a piano player strikes a piano key, a hammer hits a piano wire and makes it vibrate rapidly. As the wire moves back and forth, air molecules near it are given a push. They move a tiny distance and bounce back, but in doing so they push their neighboring molecules, which also move to and fro, and in turn push their neighbors. Eventually, the air molecules near your ear push against the eardrum and make it vibrate. These vibrations reach the nerves that go to your brain, and then you hear the sound.

Unlike light, sound cannot travel through a vacuum or the emptiness of outer space. Something is needed to carry it. Scientists have known this since 1660 when Robert Boyle found he could hear nothing after placing his watch in a jar and pumping out the air. People on the airless moon will hear no sounds except those that come to them by radio.

Air is not the only thing that can carry sound, however. Sound travels even better through water or solids. In the Old West, people pressed their ears to the rails to listen for an approaching train. The rails brought the sound quicker than did air. An Indian scout listened for the hoofbeats of distant horses by putting his ear to the ground. An outboard motor sounds much louder to a swimmer when he is underwater than when his ears are out of the water. The scratching of a pin at one end of a log can be easily heard at the other end of the log. Tapping a hammer on a water pipe in the basement is easily heard on the floor above. Many people whose eardrums have failed hear through the bones of their skull. Thomas Edison was deaf, but he heard the phonograph he invented through vibrations in his teeth.

Sound, like light, travels in waves, but it travels much slower. Light travels at the almost unbelievable speed of 186,000 miles a second. Anything we see is happening almost the instant we see it. Sound, however, travels only about 1100 feet a second. It is so slow that we can see a carpenter hammer a nail on a distant building and then have to wait for the sound to reach us.

Lightning and thunder are produced at the same time in a thunderstorm, but we first see the flash and then hear the thunder. You can figure out how far away the lightning was by counting the number of seconds between the time you see the flash and the time you hear the thunder. It takes sound about five seconds to travel one mile, so if you count 10 seconds between the flash and the thunder, you know the lightning flash was about two miles away.

Science is discovering new ways to use sound. One kind of sound that scientists use is made of waves that move so rapidly that they cannot be heard by the human ear. This kind of sound is called *ultrasound.*

Ultrasound will bounce off objects just as a man's voice will bounce off a canyon wall and cause an echo. Ultrasound is used to locate submarines hidden under the water. It is also used to locate diseases hidden deep inside the body. Doctors think it might also be used to heal wounds and to knock out pain.

Someday every home might have an ultrasonic washer that will clean dishes and clothes with sound waves. Some experimental machines have already been built. People, however, will probably have to continue to clean themselves with soap and water. Ultrasound would probably be too dangerous to use for "washing" our ears.

The Peaceful Promises
of the Atom

MILLIONS OF PEOPLE in the world go to bed hungry. One reason is that people cannot grow enough food because the land they live on is too dry. Some of this land is even near great oceans, which cover three-fourths of the earth's surface. But ocean water cannot be used to water the land because it is too salty.

Why not take the salt out of the water? Then the tons of water in the oceans could be used to turn the deserts into gardens. Until very recently, though, taking the salt out of the ocean water cost too much, because so much energy is needed. But now that men can use atomic energy, the United States and other countries would like to build atomic reactors that would *desalt* the water cheaply. Someday, if this can be accomplished, good crops could grow in what are now dry deserts, watered by ocean water with the salt taken out.

Desalting sea water is only one of the many promises of the atom. Atomic energy is beginning to play a large role in the peacetime activities of the world. The promises of the atom seem endless because it is such a powerful force. The heat produced by atomic energy is being used to drive submarines. Ships using atomic energy can go around the world 14 times without taking on more fuel. Many cities get electricity from atomic power plants. There is much that is still to be learned, but someday atomic power will be used to dig canals, harbors, and mountain passes.

There is more to the atom than just tremendous power. Some of the most important uses involve radioactive atoms called *radioisotopes*. They give off energy after they have been placed in an atomic furnace and left there for a short time.

The energy given off by radioisotopes can be used in many ways. They can be used as a kind of "super X-ray" to look inside the human body. If the radioactive atoms are mixed with food and swallowed, they can be followed through the body by the rays they give off. These rays cannot be seen or heard or felt. However, they can be detected by a Geiger counter (a machine that clicks when it is near something radioactive), and traced wherever they go. By following these atoms, scientists can tell where food goes in the blood stream.

CONTROL ROOM
OF ATOMIC-POWERED SHIP
N.S. SAVANNAH

Tracer atoms have helped doctors learn a lot about digestion. The atoms' paths through the body show how much calcium bones take up, how much iodine a thyroid gland absorbs, how well a heart is working, or where a cancer may be hidden.

Tracer atoms are also used in agriculture. They can be mixed with the soil in which plants are growing. The invisible rays can be followed up the roots and stems of the plant and into the fruit. Scientists can trace the path of fertilizer from the ground up into the plant. They can also answer such questions as how fast do roots grow,

how deep does an earthworm burrow, and how quickly does a mouthful of hay reach a cow's stomach.

Mosquitoes have been tagged with radioactive atoms to find out how far they travel from the pool in which they hatch. When they catch any of these mosquitoes, scientists can tell where they were born as surely as if the insects carried a sign around their necks. In the same way, much has been learned about the movement of flies which spread disease. Cockroaches sprayed with radioactive atoms have shown how they invade homes, even passing through water traps in the plumbing.

Businesses and factories also use tagged atoms. Automobile manufacturers can tell how much wear the piston rings in their engines get in a test run without taking the engine apart. Petroleum workers place radioisotopes between two materials, such as kerosene and gasoline, flowing in the same pipeline, to signal where the flow of one product ends and the other begins. Radioisotopes are used to measure the thicknesses of all sorts of coatings which are put on sheets of metal, floor coverings, and papers.

Scientists have found that atomic rays can destroy cancer in the thyroid gland. They give patients an "atomic cocktail" to drink. It contains radioactive iodine atoms. The iodine travels to the thyroid gland and carries the cancer-killing radiation with it.

Atomic radiation can also keep foods from spoiling. The rays destroy the bacteria that make food spoil. The food does not become radioactive because only a low dose of radiation is used. Fewer vitamins are lost this way than would be if the food were canned or frozen. Radiated food does not even need to be put in a refrigerator. You can keep it on the shelf, take it on a hike, or carry it when you go camping.

Atoms help us learn about ancient life. Thousands of years ago, living plants took in radioactive material from the air. Animals ate the plants, and the radioactive material then became part of the animals. Ancient men ate the animals. When the bones of an ancient man or animal are found, the amount of radioactivity left in them can be measured. This amount tells scientists how long ago an ancient man or animal lived.

There are still more wonders to come from the atom. Scientists think it is possible to build atomic engines that will push spaceships at fantastic speeds—much faster than the mightiest rockets we now know. It might even be possible to build small atomic engines for cars. If so, we might be able to drive for a year or more without having to stop for "gas."

Ancient Medicine

IN ANCIENT TIMES when people became ill, they believed that evil spirits, or demons, had gotten into their body. When the "medicine man" came, he brought no medicine. He came to drive the evil spirits out of the body. He recited prayers, incantations, and magic formulas. Sometimes he gave the patient a terrible-smelling concoction to eat. If the mixture was unpleasant enough, the evil spirit would go away. Or, if that didn't work, the medicine man might put on a mask and feathered headdress and paint his body with streaks of color. Then he would shout to frighten the spirits away!

Sometimes the medicine men would cut a hole into the bone of the skull to let the "demon" escape. The opening varied in size from a tiny hole up to one about two inches in diameter. Bones of men, women, and children with holes in their skulls have been found in Peru, in Egypt, and in many other parts of the world where primitive people lived. Scientists today believe that many people actually survived this kind of surgery.

Of course, this was not really medicine. It was part magic and part religion. The history of medicine really begins in ancient Sumer in the Middle East. The Sumerians wrote on clay tablets. Some tablets that have been found tell about a medical profession.

The Sumerian civilization came to an end about 2,000 years before the birth of Christ and was replaced by a new civilization, Babylonia, in the land between the Tigris and Euphrates rivers. A strict code of laws written by the Babylonian king Hammurabi was engraved on a pillar of hard black stone. Among the laws was one telling how much a doctor could charge. Another law said that if a doctor opened an infection and the patient died, the doctor's hands would be cut off!

The first ancient physician we know by name was Imhotep, who lived in Egypt. Imhotep is unusual because he is the only medical man ever to be worshipped as a god! He was worshipped as a divine physician for many hundreds of years after his death. Many temples were built in Egypt to honor him.

We know from Egyptian picture writings *(hiero-glyphics)* that they used gargles, snuffs, and drugs like hemlock and castor oil. They colored medicines to make them more attractive, and flavored or sweetened them for better taste, just as we do today. They knew the importance of cleanliness, too. Archaeologists (scientists who dig to explore ancient buried civilizations) have found washrooms in the houses of rich Egyptians.

Of course, none of the early medicine was scientific medicine. That began with the Greeks, even though Greek medicine was still mixed with religion. Apollo, the sun god, was the first god of healing. He is said to have transmitted his knowledge to his son Asclepius, to whom many temples of healing were built.

The Greek culture produced Hippocrates, a doctor called "the father of medicine." Hippocrates was a religious man, but he did not believe sickness was a punishment sent by the gods or that it could be cured by praying to the gods. At that time epilepsy was believed by most people to be a sacred disease. Hippocrates said that it was no more sacred than any other disease and that it had a natural, physical cause.

Hippocrates also said that there was nothing to magical rites. He told doctors they had to find the real cause of disease. He brought the days of the witch doctor and the magician to an end. He opened the door for the beginning of modern medicine.

Hippocrates did not believe in giving too many drugs. He said the healing forces of nature would help most patients get well. He made many medical statements that modern science has proven to be true. For

168

example, he said that fat people are more likely to die suddenly than slender people. He paid particular attention to the kinds of foods that people ate. He described the diseases that today are called mumps, pneumonia, and malaria. He pointed out that diseases occur in all seasons, but that colds, sore throats, and pneumonia are more common in winter than in summer. He said the dry seasons are more healthy than the rainy. He also wrote that the brain was the most important part of the body.

Hippocrates knew how to describe illness clearly. He kept notes about the sickness of each patient. Doctors today maintain medical charts that are patterned after Hippocrates' system. The notes are kept so that the same signs will be recognized if they are seen in another patient. The doctor can learn from his experience.

Hippocrates kept notes on patients, but he kept no notes about himself. Little is known about his life except that he was born in 460 B.C. But many of his medical statements have been collected in books written by his students and admirers.

Hippocrates would sit under the shade of a tree on his native island of Cos, and examine patients while his students looked on. According to legend, the tree still stands.

Before his students went out to practice, they were required to take an oath about their behavior as doctors. Even today, the same oath is still taken at graduation ceremonies in most medical schools. Of all the gifts the ancient Greeks gave humanity, the *Hippocratic oath* has been one of the greatest. It is an ethical code of correct conduct for doctors which has guided the practice of medicine for more than 2,000 years.

170

The next great physician after Hippocrates was Galen, who lived in Rome in the early centuries of the Christian era. He was a surgeon for the Roman gladiators and for the family of the emperor.

Galen's influence was so great that people quoted him as an authority for 1,500 years after his death. For one thing, he learned much about the bones and tissues of the body by dissecting apes and cattle. He found that there are nerves that carry the feeling of pain to the brain and separate nerves that control walking. Up to that time, people thought that the arteries contained air, but Galen proved that they were filled with blood. He also showed that the blood was moved by the pumping action of the heart.

After the fall of the Roman Empire, medicine and all other sciences were almost forgotten in the troubles of the Dark Ages. Disease was regarded as a punishment for sin that could be removed only by prayer and repentance. But many doctors kept medical knowledge alive by studying the works of Galen and of Hippocrates. They used them as a basis for their own discoveries when the science of medicine was revived in the Middle Ages, and began to move forward into modern times.

Modern Medicine

ABOUT 40 YEARS AGO, the son of President Calvin Coolidge developed an infected foot after playing tennis. He died of blood poisoning. Doctors in the 1920's did not have the right medicine to save his life.

Only a few years after that young man died, another president's son, Franklin D. Roosevelt, Jr., was rushed to the hospital with a serious infection in his throat. Newspaper reporters waited outside, expecting bad news. But Mrs. Roosevelt came out looking very happy. They were using a new medicine, and her son would be well enough to spend Christmas at home.

The new medicine was called *prontosil*. It was the first of a new group of "wonder drugs." After prontosil, one important medicine after another came tumbling out of the laboratory. Doctors began curing all kinds of infections with these drugs called "sulfas."

But better drugs were yet to come. One day, a stray mold drifted through the air and into the laboratory window of Dr. Alexander Fleming in Scotland. The mold landed on a tray in which some germs were growing. When Dr. Fleming looked at the tray later, he was startled to find that all of the germs were destroyed. The stray mold that had killed the germs was later named *penicillin*. It is one of the most important medicines ever discovered.

All of us who live in this golden age of medicine are fortunate. Before the wonder drugs were discovered, an average person could expect to live only for 45 years. Today men live for an average of 70 years, and women even longer. The poorest sick person today can be treated with much better medicines than a doctor 40 years ago could give to the family of the president of the United States.

New drugs are not the only way that medicine has given us longer and healthier lives. Doctors have learned to operate inside a living heart. Many children born with deformed hearts can now be made well. They can run and jump and play with other children instead of having to sit on the sidelines and watch.

For some operations, surgeons shut the heart off entirely. They disconnect its blood vessels, and attach them to a machine which pumps the blood through the

body. After fixing the heart, they reattach the blood vessels to the heart, and the patient is fully recovered.

Doctors today can even take out a sick heart and replace it with a healthy heart taken from a person who has died. The first *heart transplant* was done by Dr. Christiaan Barnard in Cape Town, South Africa, in 1967. Not long ago, doctors replaced the heart of a dying man with a mechanical heart. The man, whose name was Barney Clark, lived for 112 days. This experience opens up a new world of medical treatment.

Even before surgeons transplanted hearts, they learned how to transplant kidneys from one person to another. Hundreds of people are living today using kidneys that were donated to them by relatives or friends. Because people have *two* kidneys, they can give one to a person who needs it—and still stay well themselves.

Doctors say that they eventually will not have to transplant hearts or kidneys from other people. They will be able to use artificial ones of plastic or metal.

Dentists have also learned to replant teeth that have been knocked out. Sometimes completely new teeth, made of plastic, have been put in place of teeth that have been pulled.

Along with amazing new cures for illness, doctors are also discovering ways to *prevent* sickness. No longer does anyone have to suffer from a withered or shortened leg because of polio. We now have a polio vaccine that keeps children from getting the disease. There are also new vaccines to prevent mumps and measles and several other diseases. Doctors hope some day to have a vaccine that will prevent the common cold.

176

AVERAGE HEIGHT OF 10-YEAR-OLD BOYS

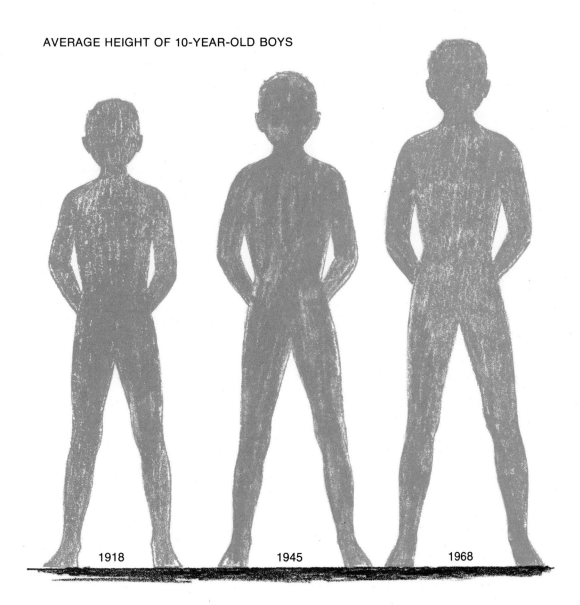

1918   1945   1968

Medicine has discovered so much about good nutrition that children today are growing stronger, taller, and heavier than their grandfathers and grandmothers. Doctors know the right amount of vitamins that the body needs to remain healthy. To make sure that everyone gets vitamins, they are put in cereal, bread, milk, and many other common foods.

With so many discoveries already made in medicine, is there anything left to do for young people who want to become doctors? There are still many problems in medicine to solve. Cancer kills thousands of people every year. So do heart disease, brain diseases, high blood pressure, and leukemia. The lives of many are miserable because they have some kind of mental illness.

With everyone living longer these days, the health problems of old people are becoming increasingly important. Doctors need to find ways to help older people enjoy their old age in greater comfort.

The greatest challenge facing medicine is to understand better the cells of our body—what makes them grow and change, and what harms them. Possibly then scientists can change or cure things that are wrong with the cells that babies inherit from their mothers and fathers. They may be able to prevent many of the birth defects that harm thousands of babies every year.

New Sciences

REMEMBER THE LAST WINTRY day you were out of doors when the temperature was zero? You may shiver just thinking of it. Imagine being in Siberia at 50 degrees below zero, on a windswept Himalayan mountain peak at 100 degrees below zero, or in the Antarctic on the day of the coldest temperature ever recorded—126.9 degrees below zero.

These cold temperatures would all be heat waves for a group of scientists who work in the strange world of *cryogenics* or "supercold." The temperatures they deal with are from minus 250 degrees to the coldest possible temperature—minus 459.7 degrees. This temperature is called *absolute zero*. At that temperature everything in the world would be frozen solid.

Scientists have found supercold to be a useful tool in space flight, medicine, and surgery. Supercold can turn oxygen and hydrogen gases into liquids. This reduces their volume and makes it possible for them to be used on spaceships as fuel. Supercold allows electricity to flow through wires with no friction to stop it. It enables doctors to store blood for many months instead of for just three weeks as in ordinary refrigerators. Surgeons can destroy a diseased spot in a human body with a cryogenic tool quicker and safer than they can with a knife.

Cryogenics might be the answer to one of the problems in traveling to the distant stars. This problem is how to enable the passengers to endure the 20- or 40-year trip. One possible solution is frozen sleep. The passengers might be put into suspended animation with cold temperatures and brought back to consciousness when they reach their destination.

At the opposite end from cryogenics is the field of superheat. At hot temperatures like those on the sun,

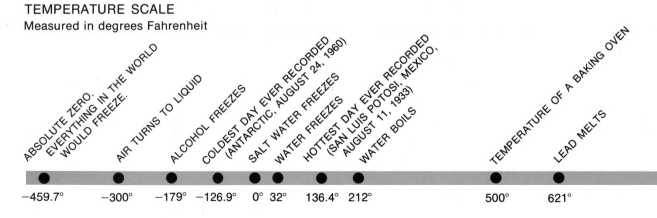

TEMPERATURE SCALE
Measured in degrees Fahrenheit

ABSOLUTE ZERO. EVERYTHING IN THE WORLD WOULD FREEZE. AIR TURNS TO LIQUID ALCOHOL FREEZES COLDEST DAY EVER RECORDED (ANTARCTIC, AUGUST 24, 1960) SALT WATER FREEZES WATER FREEZES HOTTEST DAY EVER RECORDED (SAN LUIS POTOSI, MEXICO, AUGUST 11, 1933) WATER BOILS TEMPERATURE OF A BAKING OVEN LEAD MELTS

−459.7°   −300°   −179° −126.9°   0° 32°   136.4° 212°   500°   621°

180

solid material turns into matter that is not a liquid, not a solid, and not a gas. It is so different from anything on earth that scientists call it the fourth state of matter, and have given it the name *plasma.* Even though plasma does not normally exist on earth, most of the matter in the rest of the universe is plasma. The sun and the other stars are plasma.

It is difficult even to imagine how hot plasma is. The baking oven in the kitchen reaches about 500 degrees Fahrenheit. The gas burners on the kitchen stove will reach about 3,000 degrees. Gasoline burns in our automobiles at 3,500 degrees. Until the atomic bomb was developed, the hottest temperature that had been created on earth was 7,000 degrees. The atomic bomb produces 40,000 degrees.

No solid container on earth can hold plasma. It would melt anything you put it in. Scientists try to hold it in a "magnetic bottle." They surround it with magnetic forces to keep it from escaping.

If scientists can learn to control plasma for a second or two, they would be able to use the waters of the oceans as a new type of nuclear fuel.

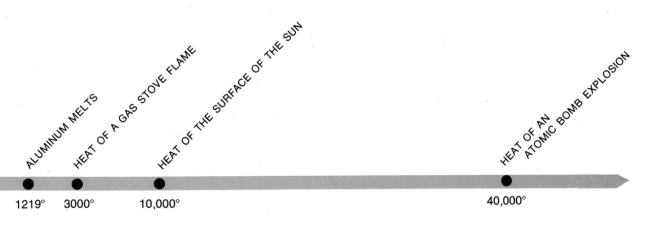

ALUMINUM MELTS — HEAT OF A GAS STOVE FLAME — HEAT OF THE SURFACE OF THE SUN — HEAT OF AN ATOMIC BOMB EXPLOSION

1219°   3000°   10,000°   40,000°

The science of *fluidics* is so new that scientists have not even agreed on how to define it. Instead of electricity flowing through wires, fluidics deals with liquids and gases moving through tiny networks of pipes or tubes. The fluid energy can be used to control a washing machine or the course of a torpedo. It will enable a big ship to turn around in a circle without moving forward.

Man's attempts to explore space have led to many new and unusual problems. Many new branches of science have been developed to try to find answers to these problems. One of these problems, oddly enough, has to do with time.

Even though you may not know what time it is as you read this page, your body does. It has a *biological clock*. It signals you when to rest and when to get up. Every other living thing in nature has a biological clock. Plants flower and produce their seed by their biological clocks. Bats know when to fly in the evening.

Biological clocks have become important to some scientists who believe that cancer or even heart attacks may occur when the body is thrown out of rhythm. They also know that our temperature is at its highest point during the day and at its lowest point between 2 o'clock and 5 o'clock in the morning. Ordinarily, we feel our best and do our best work when our temperature is highest (though not so high that we have a fever).

With our high speed jet transportation, many people arrive in Europe in the morning, but their biological clock only registers the middle of the night. It is difficult for them to do their best work.

For an astronaut whirling through space, a "day" is only about 90 minutes long. That is the length of time it takes him to go completely around the earth, passing through a day and a night. It has been found, however, that astronauts function best if they maintain the same sleep and waking cycle that they were used to on earth.

Space exploration has also forced scientists to find out how man can get used to living in an entirely new environment. There is no air in space. Man has to take along his own oxygen. There is no air pressure in space. Man has to take along his own air pressure. On earth, man is accustomed to the pull of gravity to keep him right-side-up. In space there is no gravity. Everything floats about if it is not tied down.

These problems are being investigated by doctors who are part of the new science of *space medicine*. Space doctors must protect astronauts from the harmful rays in space, insulate them against the heat when they face the sun and against the cold when they travel on the dark side of the earth.

Until recently astronomers learned most of what they know about the distant stars through what they saw in the big telescopes. Many nights they cannot see because of clouds. But the strange new science of *radio astronomy* has arisen to give them a new window on the universe. The radio telescope is not bothered by clouds. Though only an infant science, radio astronomy has made important contributions to understanding our galaxy, our sun, our neighboring planets, and our own atmosphere.

Radio astronomers use huge, dish-shaped antennae to pick up a particular kind of radiation from stars. Radio telescopes pinpoint their position in space and tell how far away they are. Some of the information they get comes from stars that have exploded and galaxies that have collided.

Inventions

INVENTION	INVENTOR	COUNTRY	DATE
Airplane	Wright Brothers	U.S.	1903
Airship (dirigible)	Zeppelin	Germany	1900
Automobile	Daimler	Germany	1887
Balloon (aviation)	Montgolfier	France	1783
Barometer	Torricelli	Italy	1643
Battery, electric	Volta	Italy	1800
Bicycle	MacMillan	Scotland	1842
Burner, gas	Bunsen	Germany	1855
Camera, Kodak	Eastman	U.S.	1888
Cash register	Ritty	U.S.	1879
Cellophane	Bradenberger	Switzerland	1900
Cement	Aspdin	England	1845
Cotton gin	Whitney	U.S.	1793
Dental plate, rubber	Goodyear	U.S.	1855

INVENTION	INVENTOR	COUNTRY	DATE
Diesel engine	Diesel	Germany	1895
Dynamite	Nobel	Sweden	1866
Electromagnet	Sturgeon	England	1824
Elevator, passenger	Otis	U.S.	1857
Evaporated milk	Borden	U.S.	1856
Flying shuttle	Kay	England	1733
Fountain pen	Waterman	U.S.	1884
Garbage disposal	Merrill	U.S.	1935
Gyroscope	Foucault	France	1852
Harvester-thresher	Matteson	U.S.	1888
Helicopter	Sikorski	U.S.	1939
Jet propulsion	Whittle	England	1930
Lawn mower	Hills	U.S.	1868
Lightning rod	Franklin	U.S.	1752
Linoleum	Walton	England	1860
Locomotive	Stephenson	England	1829
Loom, power	Cartwright	England	1785
Machine gun	Gatling	U.S.	1861
Match, friction	Walker	England	1827

INVENTION	INVENTOR	COUNTRY	DATE
Microscope	Janssen	Netherlands	1590
Motorcycle	Daimler	Germany	1885
Movies, silent	Edison	U.S.	1893
Movies, sound	Edison	U.S.	1913
Nuclear reactor	Fermi	Italy	1942
Nylon	Du Pont Lab.	U.S.	1937
Oleomargarine	Mege-Mouries	France	1868
Phonograph	Edison	U.S.	1877
Piano	Cristofori	Italy	1709
Pistol (revolver)	Colt	U.S.	1835
Printing press	Gutenberg	Germany	1450
Radar	Taylor and Young	U.S.	1922
Radio	Marconi	Italy	1895
Railroad sleeping car	Pullman	U.S.	1858
Rayon	Swan	England	1883
Reaper	McCormick	U.S.	1834
Refrigerator	Goss	U.S.	1913
Rocket engine (liquid fuel)	Goddard	U.S.	1926

INVENTION	INVENTOR	COUNTRY	DATE
Rubber, vulcanized	Goodyear	U.S.	1839
Sewing machine	Howe	U.S.	1846
Spinning jenny	Hargreaves	England	1767
Steam engine	Watt	Scotland	1769
Steamboat	Fulton	U.S.	1807
Steel	Bessemer	England	1856
Stethoscope	Laennec	France	1819
Submarine	Bushnell	U.S.	1776
Tank, military	Swinton	England	1914
Telegraph	Morse	U.S.	1837
Telephone	Bell	U.S.	1876
Telescope	Lippershey	Netherlands	1608
Television	Zworykin	U.S.	1934
Thermometer	Galileo	Italy	1593
Thermometer, mercury	Fahrenheit	Germany	1714
Torpedo	Whitehead	England	1866
Transistor	Shockley, Brattain, and Bardeen	U.S.	1948
Typewriter	Mitterhoffer	Austria	1864

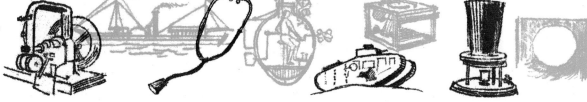

MENDEL

DOUBLEDAY

DARWIN

LAVOISIER

Discoveries and Theories

	DISCOVERER	COUNTRY	DATE
Atomic theory	Dalton	England	1803
Bacteria	Leeuwenhoek	Netherlands	1683
Baseball, game of	Doubleday	U.S.	1839
Basketball, game of	Naismith	U.S.	1891
Combustion, principle	Lavoisier	England	1777
Communism, theory of	Marx	England	1848
DDT	Zeidler	Germany	1874
Elements, table	Mendeleyev	Russia	1869
Evolution, theory of	Darwin	England	1859
Gravity, law of	Newton	England	1687
Heart transplant	Barnard	South Africa	1967
Heredity, law of	Mendel	Austria	1865
Hydrogen	Cavendish	England	1776
Insulin	Banting, Best, and MacLeod	Canada	1922

	DISCOVERER	COUNTRY	DATE
Intelligence tests (IQ's)	Binet and Simon	France	1905
Laser	Townes and Schawlow	U.S.	1958
Measles vaccine	Enders and Peebles	U.S.	1954
Nuclear reaction, controlled	Fermi	Italy	1942
Oxygen	Priestley	England	1774
Penicillin	Fleming	England	1929
Plants and animals, classification	Linnaeus	Sweden	1753
Plastics	Baekeland	Belgium/U.S.	1907
Polio vaccine	Salk	U.S.	1953
Polio vaccine (oral)	Sabin	U.S.	1955
Psychoanalysis	Freud	Austria	1904
Rabies vaccine	Pasteur	France	1885
Radioactivity	Becquerel	France	1896
Radium	Pierre Curie, Marie Curie	France Poland	1898
Relativity, theory of	Einstein	Germany	1905
Smallpox vaccine	Jenner	England	1796
Uranium	Klaproth	Germany	1789
Xerography	Carlson	U.S.	1938
X-ray	Roentgen	Germany	1895

Fact Book

Facts About Our Earth

WHETHER OUR EARTH is a big or small place depends on how you look at it. It is only one of nine planets revolving around the sun (our star). Our star is only one of trillions of stars in the universe. Our earth, just a speck in the vast universe, seems like a very tiny place.

Yet it is a pretty big place, too—over 24,000 miles around, which is equal to almost 200,000 city blocks. There are great mountains and rivers, continents covering millions of square miles, and oceans even larger than the continents. This section tells about the largest, longest, tallest, and greatest natural wonders of our earth.

The Earth

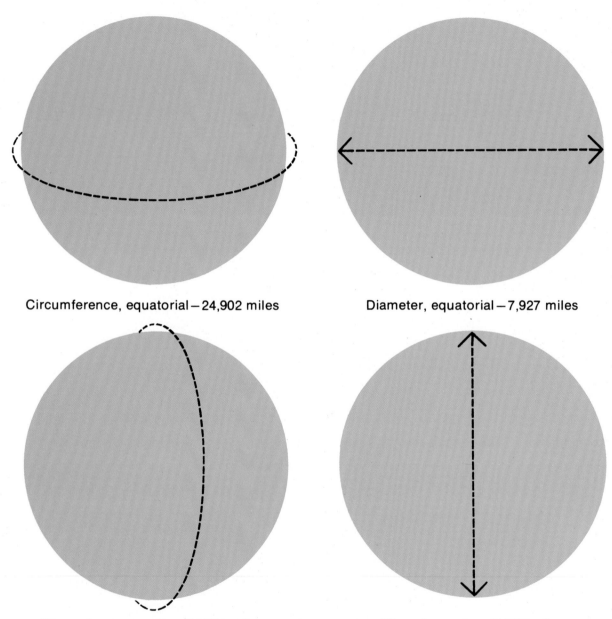

Circumference, equatorial — 24,902 miles

Diameter, equatorial — 7,927 miles

Circumference, polar — 24,861 miles

Diameter, polar — 7,900 miles

Area of land — 57,470,000 square miles

Area of water — 139,480,000 square miles

The Earth is approximately 71% water and 29% land.

The Seven Continents

Africa

area—11,500,000 square miles
rank in area—2
rank in population—3

North America

area—9,300,000 square miles
rank in area—3
rank in population—4

Europe

area—3,750,000 square miles
rank in area—6
rank in population—2

South America

area—6,800,000 square miles
rank in area—4
rank in population—5

Asia

area—16,900,000 square miles
rank in area—1
rank in population—1

Antarctica

area—5,300,000 square
miles
rank in area—5
rank in population—7

Australia

area—2,968,000 square miles
rank in area—7
rank in population—6

The Four Largest Islands in the World

Greenland
area—840,000 square miles
location—Atlantic Ocean

Borneo
area—286,900 square miles
location—Pacific Ocean

New Guinea
area—316,600 square miles
location—Pacific Ocean

Madagascar
area—226,650 square miles
location—Indian Ocean

The Five Longest Rivers in the World

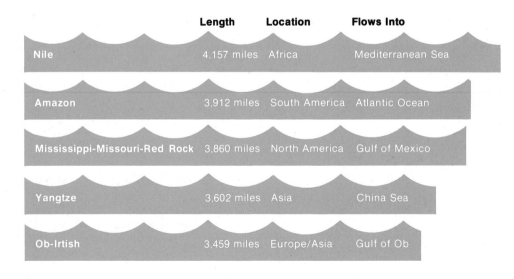

	Length	Location	Flows Into
Nile	4,157 miles	Africa	Mediterranean Sea
Amazon	3,912 miles	South America	Atlantic Ocean
Mississippi-Missouri-Red Rock	3,860 miles	North America	Gulf of Mexico
Yangtze	3,602 miles	Asia	China Sea
Ob-Irtish	3,459 miles	Europe/Asia	Gulf of Ob

The Great Deserts of the World

Desert	Location
Sahara	Africa
Great Australian	Australia
Libyan	Africa
Gobi	Asia
Kalahari	Africa
Taklamakan	Asia
Nubian	Africa
Kara-Kum	Asia
Kyzyl-Kum	U.S.S.R.
Great Arabian	Saudi Arabia

The Four Oceans

Pacific Ocean

area—63,802,000 square miles
average depth—14,048 feet
deepest point—36,198 feet

Atlantic Ocean

area—31,839,000 square miles
average depth—12,880 feet
deepest point—30,246 feet

Indian Ocean

area—28,356,000 square miles
average depth—13,002 feet
deepest point—24,460 feet

Arctic Ocean

area—5,440,000 square miles
average depth—3,953 feet
deepest point—18,456 feet

The deepest man has ever gone in an ocean is 35,802 feet (over 6 3/4 miles). Dr. Jacques Piccard and Lt. Donald Walsh made the descent in the U.S. Navy's *bathyscaphe* "Trieste." The descent was into the Mariana Trench in the Pacific Ocean.

197

The Five Largest Seas

Malay Sea*
area — 3,144,000 square miles
average depth — 3,976 feet

South China Sea
area — 1,146,000 square miles
average depth — 5,400 feet

Caribbean Sea
area — 1,063,000 square miles
average depth — 8,685 feet

Mediterranean Sea
area — 966,750 square miles
average depth — 4,878 feet

Bering Sea
area — 875,750 square miles
average depth — 4,714 feet

*The Malay Sea includes all of the
waters south of China between
the Pacific and Indian Oceans.

The Great Lakes

The Great Lakes in North America together form
the largest body of fresh water in the world.

Lake Huron
area — 23,010 square miles
deepest point — 750 feet

Lake Ontario
area — 7,520 square miles
deepest point — 778 feet

Lake Superior
area — 31,820 square miles
deepest point — 1,333 feet

Lake Michigan
area — 22,400 square miles
deepest point — 923 feet

Lake Erie
area — 9,930 square miles
deepest point — 210 feet

198

The Largest Countries in the World

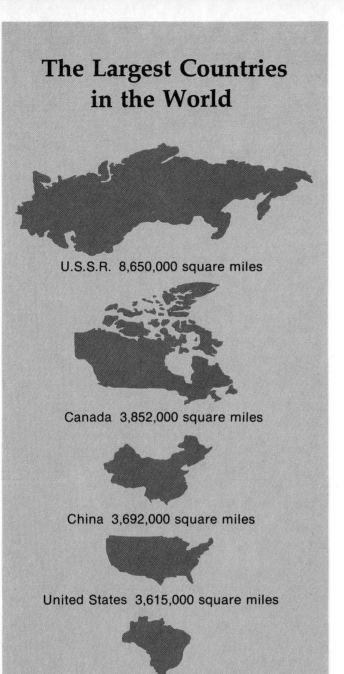

U.S.S.R. 8,650,000 square miles

Canada 3,852,000 square miles

China 3,692,000 square miles

United States 3,615,000 square miles

Brazil 3,287,000 square miles

Australia 2,968,000 square miles

India 1,176,000 square miles

Argentina 1,072,000 square miles

The Smallest Countries in the World

Vatican City State	.17 square mile
Monaco	.58 square mile
San Marino	24.00 square miles
Liechtenstein	61.00 square miles

●

Waterfalls

The Highest

Waterfall	Height	Country
Angel	3,212 feet	Venezuela
Tugela	3,110 feet	South Africa
Yosemite	2,425 feet	United States
Cuquenán	2,000 feet	Venezuela
Sutherland	1,904 feet	New Zealand

The Largest

Guaíra Falls	Brazil-Paraguay

(The Guaíra Falls dump an average of 470,000 cubic feet of water each second. The largest flow of the Guaíra is over 1,750,000 cubic feet of water each second.)

199

Highest Recorded Temperatures

In the World
136.4 degrees (in the shade) at Azizia, Libya, and also at San Luis Potosi, Mexico.

In the United States
134 degrees (in the shade) at Death Valley, California.

Lowest Recorded Temperatures

In the World
−126.9 degrees (below zero) at Vostok, Antarctica.

In the United States
−79.8 degrees (below zero) at Prospect Creek, Alaska.

Most Rainfall in the World

Mount Waialeale, Hawaii
averaging 460 inches of rain per year.

Least Rainfall in the World

Calama, Atacama Desert, Chile
No rain has ever been recorded.

200

The Highest Mountains

In The World

Mountain	Height	Country
Everest	29,028 feet	Nepal/Tibet
Godwin-Austen	28,250 feet	India/Kashmir
Kanchejunga	28,168 feet	Nepal/Sikkim
Lhotse	27,923 feet	Nepal/Tibet
Makalu	27,790 feet	Nepal/Tibet

On Each Continent

Continent	Mountain	Height	Country
Asia	Everest	29,028 feet	Nepal/Tibet
South America	Aconcagua	22,834 feet	Argentina
North America	McKinley	20,320 feet	United States
Africa	Kilimanjaro	19,340 feet	Tanzania
Europe	Elbrus	18,481 feet	U.S.S.R.
Antarctica	Vinson-Massif	16,860 feet	-------------------
Australia	Kosciusko	7,316 feet	-------------------

Trees of the World

Tallest — Redwood-367.8 feet
Redwood Creek Grove, California
(The tallest trees in the world are redwoods and are found only in northern California and southern Oregon.)

Broadest — Montezuma Cypress
Tule, Mexico
(The Montezuma cypress tree has a circumference of 160 feet around the bottom of its trunk.)

Oldest — Bristlecone Pine-4,600 years old
California
(Trees are the oldest "living" things on earth.)

Lowest Areas in the World

In Each Continent

Continent	Area	Feet Below Sea Level
Asia	Dead Sea-Israel/Jordan	1,290
Africa	Lake Assal-Ethiopia	512
North America	Death Valley-United States	282
South America	Salinas Grandes-Argentina	131
Europe	Caspian Sea-U.S.S.R.	96
Australia	Lake Eyre	39
Antarctica	------------------------------	0

201

202

People and Their Ways

THOUSANDS OF YEARS AGO, the lives of men were much different from what they are today. As time went by, people spread out across the earth—learning new things, beginning new civilizations, and gradually creating our modern world.

Today, almost 3½ billion people live on our earth in large cities, towns, and farm areas. All are important human beings in a world with many different ways of life. In this section is an outline of important events in the history of people, and facts about world populations, languages, and even some organizations for young people.

203

The Story of Man

The story of Man is full of events, discoveries, wars, great movements, and the rise and fall of civilizations. By studying the great events of the past we can understand better how the world of today came to be the way it is.

Important events of history are listed here in *chronological* order, that is, in the order in which they happened. Within each time period these events are further organized by region.

5000–3000 B.C.

Middle East

Tigris-Euphrates Valley (Iraq) is settled (5000)
Cities in Sumer (Iran) are built (3700)
Sumerians develop *cuneiform* writing (3100)

Africa

Civilized settlements in Nile Valley (Egypt-5000)
Egyptians develop *hieroglyphic* writing (3100)

Asia

People from the Asian mainland migrate to Japan (4000)
Civilized settlements begin in the Indus Valley, India (3100)

Europe

Minoan settlements begin on the island of Crete (4000)

3000–1000 B.C.

Middle East

Babylonian Empire begins (2600)
Phoenicians settle on the coast of Syria (2500)
Babylonian King Hammurabi writes Code of Laws to govern his empire (2050)
Trading begins on the Mediterranean Sea (1825)
Hittite Empire in Turkey and Syria develops (1700)
Abraham leads the Hebrews (1550)
Hittites develop iron weapons (1400)
Hittite empire falls (1100)

Africa

Egypt is unified by King Menes (3000)
The great pyramids of Egypt are built (2400)
The flight *(Exodus)* of Hebrews from Eygpt (1290)

Asia

Hsia Dynasty in China (2200-1700)
Shang Dynasty in China (1700-1050)
Chou Dynasty begins in China (1050)

Europe

Asians migrate to Greece (2900)
Age of Minoan culture on Crete; Minoans develop hieroglyphic writing (2000-1400)
Greeks conquer Troy in Trojan War (1200)
Crete falls to the Greek Dorian invasion (1100)

North America

Pueblo Indian culture begins (1450)

1000–500 B.C.

Middle East

David becomes King of Israel (1000)
Solomon succeeds David as leader of the Hebrews (950)
Assyrian Empire begins (900)
New Assyrian Empire begins with the conquering of Babylon (745)

Greeks settle in part of Italy (735)

Zoroaster, a Persian, preaches the religion of the Magi (660)

Chaldean Empire begins with the capture of Nineveh (606)

Cyrus the Great establishes the Persian Empire (539)

Africa
Carthage (Tunisia) is founded (800)
Carthaginian Empire begins (575)
Egypt is conquered by Persia (525)

Asia
Religion of Hinduism begins to develop in India (950)
Caste system is developed in India (775)
Buddha establishes his religion in India (526)
Confucius forms his *philosophy* in China (510)

Europe
Greek city-states come into being (900)
In Greece, Homer writes *The Iliad* and *The Odyssey* (875)
Rome is founded (753)

South and Central America
Mayas settle in Central America (1000)
Indian settlements are made in the Andes Mountains (550)

500–1 B.C.

Middle East
Persia controls the Middle East and Egypt (500-400)
Persia falls to the Greek armies of Alexander the Great; the Persian Empire collapses (331)
Middle East is invaded by Rome (75)
Jesus Christ is born in Judea (4)

Africa
Egypt gains its freedom from Persia (410)
Egypt falls to Alexander the Great (332)
Punic Wars between Carthage and Rome begin (264)
Hannibal leads the Carthaginians (221)
Carthage is destroyed by Rome (146)
Cleopatra is Queen of Egypt (60)

Asia
Maurya Empire in India (320-190)
Asoka the Great is ruler of India (274)
Great Wall of China is built (214)
Han Dynasty begins in China (202)
Andhra Empire in India begins (180)
Buddhism is brought to China (100)

Europe
The Golden Age of Greece (500-400)
Persian Wars between Greece and Persia (490-479)
First Peloponnesian War between Athens and Sparta (460-445)
Alexander the Great's empire stretches from Persia to Egypt to India (336-323)
Hannibal crosses the Alps into Italy (216)
Rome ends the Punic Wars by defeating Carthage (201)
Germanic tribes begin to form (150)
Julius Caesar leads the Romans to victory over Gaul (58-51)
Roman Empire is established under Augustus Caesar (27)

1 A.D.–400 A.D.

Middle East
Jesus Christ is crucified, and the age of Christianity begins (30)
Jerusalem is destroyed by the Romans (70)
Sassanian Empire begins in Persia (226)
Axumite kingdom rules Arabia (350)

Asia
Paper is invented in China (110)
Religion of Taoism is introduced in China (150)
Polynesians migrate to the Pacific Islands (200)
Gupta Empire is established in India (300)
Hun and Mongol Empires begin in China (350)

Europe
Romans control the largest block of territory in the history of the world (27-400)
Britain is conquered by Rome (50)
Nero rules Rome (54)
Great Plague devastates Europe and Asia (164-180)
Constantine rules the Roman Empire (306)
Roman Empire is divided (395)

North America

Mayan settlements in Mexico (120)

South and Central America

Mayan Empire begins in Central America (350)

400–800 A.D.

Middle East

Mohammed develops the religion of Islam (570-632)
Moslem Empire begins (622)
Moslems conquer Spain and North Africa (725)

Asia

Attila leads the Hun invasion of Europe (450)
Buddhism is introduced in Japan (552)
Tang Dynasty begins in China (618)
Moslems invade India (700)
Kyoto becomes the capital of Japan (800)

Europe

Germanic tribes settle Europe (Franks, Goths, Visigoths, Vandals, and Burgundians) (425)
Rome falls and Middle Ages begin (476)
Britain is invaded by the Angles, Saxons, and Jutes (500)
Franks are united by Clovis I (500)
Lombard Empire rules Italy (566)
Carolingian Dynasty is begun in France by Pepin (630)
Charles Martel rules the Frankish Empire (721)

800–1200 A.D.

Middle East

Moslem Empire is invaded by Charlemagne the Great (800)
Jerusalem is captured by the First Crusade (1099)
Omar Khayyam writes poetry in Persia (1100)
Saladin is Sultan of Egypt (1169)
The crusaders invade the Middle East (1200)

Asia

Angkor (in Cambodia) becomes the capital of the Khmer people (890)
Tang dynasty in China ends (907)

Europe

Charlemagne becomes Emperor of the Frankish Empire (800)

Alfred the Great unites England (871-899)
Holy Roman Empire is founded by Otto I (962)
Normans, under William the Conqueror, rule England after the Battle of Hastings (1066)
El Cid leads the forces of Spain (1094)
First Crusade sets out (1095)
Frederick Barbarossa is crowned Holy Roman Emperor (1152)

North America

Vikings explore the east coast of North America (1000)
Aztec Indians begin settlements in Mexico (1100)

1200–1600 A.D.

Middle East

Ottoman Empire begins in Turkey (1299)
Ottoman Turks take Constantinople (Istanbul) and Byzantine Empire falls (1453)
Suleiman the Magnificent expands the Ottoman Empire (1525)

Africa

Portuguese migrate to Africa (1475)
North Africa is ruled by the Ottoman Turks (1525)

Asia

Genghis Khan leads the Mongols and captures Peking, China (1214)
Kublai Khan rules the Mongols (1260)
Mongol Empire begins (1280)
Marco Polo visits China (1290)
Ming Dynasty in China (1368-1644)
Khmers fall from power in Southeast Asia (1431)
Vasco Da Gama sails around Africa to India (1498)
Sikh religion is established in India (1520)
Magellan reaches the South Pacific (1520)

Europe

"Children's Crusade"—armies of boys join the Fourth Crusade to the Holy Land (1212)
Magna Carta is signed in England (1215)
Inquisition begins in Italy (1215)
Dante writes the *Divine Comedy* in Italy (1310)
Hundred Years' war between France and England (1337-1453)

Great Plague (Black Death) spreads through Europe (1348)

Chaucer writes poetry in England (1375)

Joan of Arc leads the French armies (1429)

Leonardo Da Vinci, artist and inventor, is born in Italy (1452)

The Renaissance begins in Europe (1453)

Wars of the Roses begin in England (1455)

Copernicus shows that the earth moves around the sun (1473-1543)

Michelangelo, painter and sculptor, lives in Italy (1475-1564)

Martin Luther founds the Lutheran religion in Germany (1521)

The Reformation begins in Europe (1525)

Henry VIII, King of England, founds the Church of England (1530)

Shakespeare writes in England (1564-1616)

Galileo proves Copernicus' theory of the solar system (1564-1642)

Peter Paul Rubens paints in Europe (1577-1640)

England defeats the Spanish Armada (1588)

North America

Mexico City is founded by the Aztec Indians (1325)

Columbus crosses the Atlantic Ocean and lands in America (1492)

Mexico falls to Cortez (1520)

Sir Walter Raleigh sails to Virginia (1584)

South America

Inca Indian civilization in Peru begins (1250)

Brazil is settled by the Portuguese (1530)

Pizarro conquers the Incas (1535)

1600–1800 A.D.

Asia

Japan is closed to Europeans; Tokyo becomes the capital (1638)

Ming Dynasty in China ends, and Manchu Dynasty begins (1644)

Australia

English settlement is made at Sydney (1787)

Europe

Rembrandt paints in Holland (1606-1669)

John Milton, poet, lives in England (1608-1674)

Thirty Years' War involves all of Europe (1618-1648)

Isaac Newton, scientist and mathematician, works in England. (1642-1727)

Oliver Cromwell governs England after King Charles I is beheaded (1650)

Johann Sebastian Bach composes music in Germany (1685-1750)

Peter the Great rules Russia (1689-1725)

Mozart composes music in Austria (1756-1791)

Catherine the Great rules Russia (1762-1796)

Ludwig van Beethoven composes music in Germany (1770-1827)

Industrial Revolution in England begins (1770)

England goes to war with the American colonies (1775)

French Revolution begins (1789)

France becomes a Republic (1792)

North America

First English settlement is made at Jamestown, Virginia (1607)

Pilgrims land at Plymouth Rock (1620)

Exploration of North America (1625-1700)

French and Indian War (1754-1763)

English General James Wolfe captures Quebec (1759)

Canada is ceded to the British (1762)

Declaration of Independence is signed (1776)

Revolutionary War ends (1783)

U.S. Constitution is ratified (1789)

1800–Present

Middle East

Suez Canal is built (1869)

Oil is discovered and developed (1915)

Saudi Arabia becomes independent (1922)

Israel wins independence (1948)

Suez Canal closed in Arab-Israeli war (1967)

United Nations negotiates Arab-Israeli cease-fire (1970)

Arab states subsidize Egypt to keep the Suez Canal closed (1972)

Arab-Israeli conflict triggers world energy crisis (1973)

Friction between Christians and Muslims in Lebanon led to civil war (1975)

Anwar al-Sadat of Egypt makes bold peace gesture by visiting Jerusalem to meet with Menahem Begin of Israel (1977)

Political and economic struggles continue to cause unrest throughout all the countries of the Middle East (1977)

Middle East Peace accord agreed upon in historic meeting between Anwar al-Sadat of Egypt, Menahem Begin of Israel, and U.S. President James Earl Carter at Camp David, Maryland (1978), but unrest continues after assassination of Sadat (1980)

Africa

French control of Algeria begins (1848)

Egypt is controlled by England (1881-1922)

European colonies are established (1885)

Union of South Africa is established (1910)

African nations gain independence: Libya (1951), Sudan (1955), Morocco and Tunisia (1956), Ghana (1957), Nigeria (1960), Tanzania, Malawi and Zambia (1964), and Rhodesia (1965)

Biafra secedes from Nigeria, civil war begins (1967)

First human heart transplant is performed in South Africa (1967)

Biafra is defeated by Nigeria (1970)

Portugal, the last remaining European country to have African holdings, gives independence to its colonies (1975)

Asia

Opium wars in China (1839)

Japan is opened to the world (1865)

Japanese war with China (1894-1895)

Boxer Rebellion begins in China (1900)

Korea is annexed to Japan (1910)

Republic of China established (1912)

Gandhi uses passive resistance to gain reforms and freedom for India (1919-1948)

Japan attacks U.S. at Pearl Harbor (1941)

Atom bombs cause Japanese surrender (1945)

India and Pakistan gain their independence from England (1947)

China becomes a communist state (1948)

The Republic of Korea is formed (1948)

Korean War (1950-1953)

Vietnamese forces overthrow French rule (1954)

United states begins aid to South Vietnam (1955)

Federation of Malaysia is formed (1963)

Vietnam peace talks begin in Paris (1968)

East Pakistan gains freedom from Pakistan and becomes Bangladesch (1971)

Communist China replaces Nationalist China in United Nations (1971)

Japan and China agree to end state of war between them since 1937 (1972)

Vietnam truce signed (1973)

India tests its first nuclear bomb (1974)

North and South Vietnam become one nation (1976)

Red China and the United States establish diplomatic relations (1978)

Australia

Confederation of Australia is established (1900)

Fought with Allies in World Wars I and II (1918, 1939)

First space satellite launched for weather research (1967)

Treaty of friendship and cooperation signed with Japan (1977)

Continuing cooperation with United States shown by Prime Minister John Frazer's visit to President Gerald Ford in Washington, D.C. (1977)

Europe

Napoleon becomes Emperor of France (1804)

Napoleon's empire collapses after defeat at Waterloo (1815)

Queen Victoria rules England (1837-1901)

England and France oppose Russia in the Crimean War (1854-1856)

Sigmund Freud publishes works on psychoanalysis (1856-1939)

Charles Darwin publishes the theory of evolution (1859)

Impressionism, the first movement of modern painting, is developed in France (1862-1880)

Albert Einstein publishes relativity theory (1905)

World War I engulfs all of Europe (1914-1918)

Bolshevik Revolution succeeds in Russia (1917)

Germany and Austria surrender at Versailles, France, to end World War I (1918)

Mussolini rules Italy (1921)

Union of Soviet Socialist Republics (U.S.S.R.) is formed (1922)

Republic of Spain established (1931)

Adolf Hitler comes to power in Germany (1933)

Spanish Civil War (1936-1939)

World War II involves all of Europe (1939-1945)

Germany is defeated to end World War II (1945)

U.S.S.R. becomes the second country to develop nuclear weapons (1949)

North Atlantic Treaty Organization (NATO) is formed (1949)

U.S.S.R. launches the first satellite to orbit the earth, Sputnik I (1957)

European Economic Community (Common Market) is formed (1957)

U.S.S.R. sends the first man into orbit around the earth (1961)

East Germany constructs wall between East and West Berlin (1961)

Big Four allies of World War II, East and West Germany sign pact for free traffic between West Germany and West Berlin (1971)

Factions in Northern Ireland fight (1971)

Great Britain assumes direct rule over Northern Ireland (1972)

Free elections in Spain (1977)

Euro-Communism gains strength, particularly in Spain, France, and Italy (1978)

Queen Elizabeth II of England celebrates 25 years as monarch (1977)

Strikes in Poland, Solidarity movement (1980)

South America and Central America

Statesman-soldier Simon Bolivar helps liberate Venezuela (1811), Colombia (1821), Ecuador (1822) and Peru (1825)

Pan-American Union established (1889)

Panama Canal is completed (1914)

Chaco War between Bolivia and Paraguay (1932-1935)

Organization of American States (OAS) is formed (1948)

Chile becomes first country to publicly elect a Communist government (1970)

Chile's leftist government ousted by coup (1973)

Peron elected president of Argentina (1973)

U.S. signs 2 treaties with Panama regarding the function of the Panama Canal until 1999, and the neutrality of the waterway thereafter (1978)

Military takes over in Argentina (1976)

Civil war in El Salvador, after coup (1979)

Sandinistas take over in Nicaragua (1979)

Argentina invades Falkland Islands and is defeated by Great Britain (1982)

North America

Louisiana Purchase expands the U.S. (1803)

United States fights England in the War of 1812

Exploration and settlement of western lands in the United States (1826-1900)

Mark Twain, writer and humorist, lives in the U.S. (1835-1910)

United States Civil War (1861-1865)

Emancipation Proclamation of Abraham Lincoln frees the slaves in the U.S. (1863)

Maximilian rules Mexico (1864-1867)

Spanish-American War (1898)

United States enters World War I (1917)

Dominion of Canada is formed (1926)

Charles Lindbergh makes the first non-stop flight across the Atlantic Ocean (1927)

Great Depression begins in the U.S. (1929)

United States enters World War II (1941)

World War II ends with the surrender of Germany and Japan (1945)

United Nations is formed (1945)

United States enters Korean War (1950)

Korean truce signed (1953)

First U.S. manned satellite launched (1962)

President John F. Kennedy is assassinated in Dallas, Texas (1963)

United States lands first men on moon (1969)

President Nixon visits Russia and mainland China (1972)

U.S. and Russia agree to cooperate on health, environmental, and space projects (1972)

Apollo moon probe program completed (1972)

Richard M. Nixon becomes first U.S. President to resign office (1974)

Final U.S. Troops removed from South Vietnam (1975)

U.S. celebrates Bicentennial—200th Birthday (1976)

Summer Olympic Games in Montreal, Canada (1977)

Canada celebrates 110th year (1978)

Populations

The World	4,313,400,000

The Continents

Asia	2,559,200,000
Europe	685,800,000
Africa	457,000,000
North America	363,000,000
South America	234,000,000
Australia	14,400,000
Antarctica	0

The Five Largest Countries

China	1,080,000,000
India	640,000,000
U.S.S.R.	259,151,000
United States	219,484,000
Indonesia	143,280,000

The Ten Largest Cities in the World

Shanghai, China	10,820,000
Tokyo, Japan	9,012,000
New York, U.S.	7,896,000
Greater London, England	7,764,000
Peking, China	7,570,000
Moscow, U.S.S.R.	6,942,000
Bombay, India	5,970,575
Sao Paulo, Brazil	5,685,000
Cairo, Egypt	4,961,000
Rio de Janeiro, Brazil	4,315,746

The Ten Largest Cities in the United States

New York, New York	7,896,000
Chicago, Illinois	3,367,000
Los Angeles, California	2,810,000
Philadelphia, Pennsylvania	1,949,000
Detroit, Michigan	1,511,000
Houston, Texas	1,233,000
Baltimore, Maryland	906,000
Dallas, Texas	844,000
Washington, D.C.	757,000
Indianapolis, Indiana	745,000

The Ten Languages Most Often Spoken

Language	Areas Where Spoken	Number of People Speaking It
Mandarin	China	555,000,000
English	United Kingdom, British Commonwealth, Ireland, United States	350,000,000
Hindustani	India, Pakistan	230,000,000
Spanish	Spain, Latin America	220,000,000
Russian	Soviet Union	192,000,000
Arabic	Middle East	150,000,000
Portuguese	Portugal, Brazil	110,000,000
Japanese	Japan	107,000,000
German	Germany, Austria, Switzerland	105,000,000
Bengali	Bangladesh, India	95,000,000

This is "Hello" in each of these languages

Language	How to Write It	How to Say It
Mandarin	好	HOW
English	Hello	heh-LO
Hindustani	नमस्ते	nah-mah-STAY
Spanish	Qué tal	kay-TAHL
Russian	Здравствуйте	zh-DRAHV-zhvoo-yeh-cheh
Arabic	أهلاً وسهلاً	ah-lahn wahs-ah-lahn
	السلام عليكم	ahl sahl-am ah-LAY koom
Portuguese	Como vai	ko-mo VAH-ee
Japanese	今日わ	ko-NEE chee-WAH
German	Guten tag	goo-ten TAHK
Bengali	নমস্কার	nay-may-SKAHR

211

Ten Outstanding Organizations for Young People

Boy Scouts of America

Activities	Outdoor Education, Physical Fitness, Crafts, Nature Study, Citizenship
Age Limit	Cub Scouts (8-10) Boy Scouts (11-13) Explorer Scouts (14-17)
Address	New Brunswick, New Jersey
Magazine	*Boy's Life*

Boys' Clubs of America

Activities	Sports, Arts and Crafts, Social Functions, Vocational Training
Age Limit	7-20
Address	771 First Avenue, New York, N.Y.

Camp Fire Girls

Activities	Homemaking, Arts and Crafts, Outdoor Education, Community Service
Age Limit	Bluebirds (7-8) Camp Fire Girls (9-11) Junior Hi Camp Fire Girls (12-13) Horizon Club (14-18)
Address	65 Worth Street, New York, N.Y.
Magazine	*The Camp Fire Girls*

Little League Baseball

Activities	Organized baseball leagues
Age Limit	Little League (9-12) Senior Division (13-15)
Address	Williamsport, Pennsylvania

World Pen Pals

Activities	Exchanging letters with children in other parts of the world
Age Limit	None
Address	World Affairs Center University of Minnesota Minneapolis, Minnesota

Young Men's Christian Association (YMCA)

Activities	Sports, Arts and Crafts, Physical Fitness, Social Functions, Community Service
Age Limit	None
Address	National Council of YMCA's 291 Broadway New York, New York

Young Women's Christian Association (YWCA)

Activities	Arts and Crafts, Social Functions, Sports, Outdoor Education
Age Limit	None
Address	600 Lexington Avenue New York, New York

4-H Clubs

Activities	Farming, Livestock Raising, Community Service, Homemaking
Age Limit	10-19
Address	Federal Extension Service U.S. Department of Agriculture Washington, D. C.

Girls' Clubs of America

Activities	Arts and Crafts, Homemaking, Sports and Games, Social Functions
Age Limit	6-16
Address	101 Park Avenue, New York, N.Y.

Girl Scouts of the U.S.A.

Activities	Arts and Crafts, Homemaking, Nature Study, Citizenship
Age Limit	Brownies (7-8) Junior Girl Scouts (9-11) Cadette Girl Scouts (12-14) Senior Girl Scouts (15-17)
Address	830 Third Avenue, New York, N.Y.
Magazine	*American Girl*

213

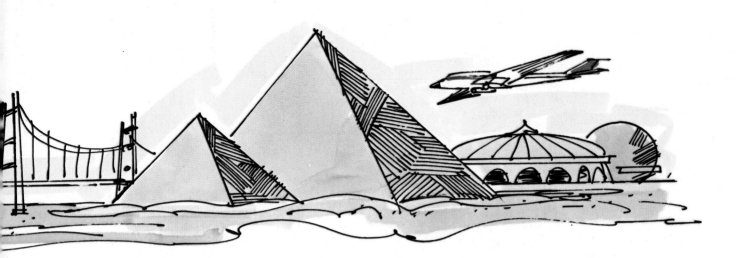

What Man Has Done

MEN HAVE DEVELOPED many wonderful things—airplanes, automobiles, electricity, television, highways, bridges, huge buildings, and fine schools. Men have made rockets to go to the moon, produced beautiful works of art, and made great discoveries in medicine.

Man has also waged bloody wars, and constructed weapons powerful enough to destroy the world. With all the knowledge and power man has gained, he now has the choice of using it to improve life on earth or completely destroy it. This section lists many of the great things men have already accomplished in our world.

The Seven Wonders of the World

	Location	Date Built (approximately)
Pyramids of Egypt*	Giza, Egypt	2580 B.C.
Hanging Gardens of Babylon	Iraq	600 B.C.
Colossus of Rhodes	Island of Rhodes (off the coast of Turkey)	280 B.C.
Temple of Artemis (Diana)	Ephesus, Turkey	350 B.C.
Tomb at Halicarnassus	Bodrum, Turkey	325 B.C.
Lighthouse of Alexandria	Island of Pharos (off the coast of Egypt)	300 B.C.
Statue of Zeus (Jupiter)	Olympia, Greece	500 B.C.

*The Pyramids of Egypt are the only one of the Seven Wonders of the World still in existence.

The Largest Buildings in the World

	Floor Area	Stories	Location	Date Built
Pentagon	6,500,000 square feet	5	Arlington, Virginia	1943
Sears Tower	4,500,000 square feet	110	Chicago, Illinois	1974
Merchandise Mart	4,023,400 square feet	25	Chicago, Illinois	1931

The Tallest Buildings in the World

	Height	Stories	City	Completion Date
Sears Tower	1,454 feet	110	Chicago	1974
World Trade Center	1,353 feet	110	New York	1972
Empire State Building	1,250 feet	102	New York	1931
Standard Oil Building	1,136 feet	80	Chicago	1972

The Longest Ship Canal in the World

	Location	Length
Suez Canal	Egypt	100.6 miles

The Longest Seaway in the World

	Location	Length
St. Lawrence Seaway	United States-Canada	189 miles

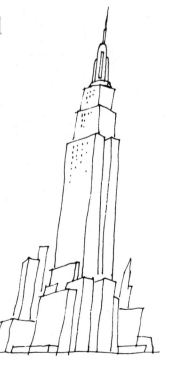

The Tallest Dams in the World

	Location	Height
Grand Dixence	Switzerland	932 feet
Mica	Canada	794 feet
Chivor	Colombia	778 feet

The Largest Dam in the World

	Location	Consists of
Tarbela	Pakistan	186,000,000 cubic yards of earth and rock

Type of Bridge	Bridge	Location	Length
The Longest *Suspension* Bridge	Mackinac Straits	Mackinaw City-St. Ignace, Michigan	7,400 foot total span
The Longest *Single Span* Bridge	Verrazano-Narrows	New York City	4,260 foot center span
The Longest *Highway* Bridge	Lake Pontchartrain Causeway	New Orleans	24 miles
The Longest *Steel Arch* Bridge	Bayonne (Kill Van Kull)	Bayonne, New Jersey	1,652 foot span
The Longest *Cantilever* Bridge	Quebec (Railway)	Quebec, Canada	1,800 foot span
The *Highest* Bridge	Royal Gorge	Arkansas River, Colorado	**Height Above Water** 1,053 feet
The *Oldest* Bridge (still in existence)	Meles River	İzmir (Smyrna), Turkey	**Date Built** 850 B.C.

Nobel Peace Prize Awards

Schweitzer

Bunche

Year		Country
1901	Jean Henry Dunant,	Switzerland
	Frédéric Passy	France
1902	Elie Ducommun,	Switzerland
	Charles Albert Gobat	Switzerland
1903	Sir William R. Cremer	England
1904	Institute of International Law	Belgium
1905	Baroness Bertha von Suttner	Austria
1906	Theodore Roosevelt	United States
1907	Ernesto Teodora Moneta,	Italy
	Louis Renault	France
1908	Klas Pontus Arnoldson,	Sweden
	Fredrik Bajer	Denmark
1909	Auguste Beernaert,	Belgium
	Baron d'Estournelles de Constant	France
1910	International Peace Bureau	Switzerland
1911	Tobias Asser	Netherlands
	Alfred Fried	Austria
1912	Elihu Root	United States
1913	Henri la Fontaine	Belgium
1917	International Red Cross	Switzerland
1919	Woodrow Wilson	United States
1920	Léon Bourgeois	France
1921	Karl Hjalmar Branting,	Sweden
	Christian Louis Lange	Norway
1922	Fridtjof Nansen	Norway
1925	Sir Joseph Austen Chamberlain,	England
	Charles Gates Dawes	United States
1926	Aristide Briand,	France
	Gustav Stresemann	Germany
1927	Ferdinand Buisson,	France
	Ludwig Quidde	Germany
1929	Frank B. Kellogg	United States
1930	Nathan Söderblom	Sweden
1931	Jane Addams,	United States
	Nicholas Murray Butler	United States

(Missing dates indicate years in which Peace Prize was not awarded.)

1933	Sir Norman Angell	England
1934	Arthur Henderson	England
1935	Carl von Ossietzky	Germany
1936	Carlos Saavedra Lamas	Argentina
1937	Viscount Cecil of Chelwood	England
1938	Nansen International Office for Refugees	Switzerland
1944	International Red Cross	Switzerland
1945	Cordell Hull	United States
1946	Emily Greene Balch,	United States
	John R. Mott	United States
1947	American Friends Service Committee,	United States
	Friends Service Council	England
1949	Lord Boyd-Orr	England
1950	Ralph Bunche	United States
1951	Léon Jouhaux	France
1952	Albert Schweitzer	Africa
1953	George C. Marshall	United States
1954	Office of the United Nations High Commissioner for Refugees	- - - - -
1957	Lester B. Pearson	Canada
1958	Dominique Georges Pire, O.P.	Belgium
1959	Philip J. Noel-Baker	England
1960	Albert John Luthuli	Africa
1961	Dag Hammarskjold	Sweden
1962	Linus C. Pauling	United States
1963	International Red Cross,	Switzerland
	League of Red Cross Societies	Switzerland
1964	Dr. Martin Luther King	United States
1965	United Nations Children's Fund (UNICEF)	- - - - -
1968	René Cassin	France
1969	International Labor Organization	- - - - -
1970	Norman E. Borlaug	United States
1971	Willy Brandt	West Germany
1973	Henry Kissinger	United States
	Le Duc Tho	North Vietnam
1974	Sean MacBride	Ireland
	Eisaku Sato	Japan
1975	Andrei D. Sakharov	U.S.S.R.
1976	Mairead Corrigan	Ireland
	Betty Williams	Ireland
1977	Amnesty International	England
1978	Anwar al-Sadat	Egypt
	Menahem Begin	Israel
1979	Mother Theresa of Calcutta	Yugoslavia
1980	Adolfo Pérez Esquivel	Argentina
1981	Office of the United Nations High Commissioner for Refugees	- - - - -
1982	Alfonso Garcia Robles	Mexico
	Alva Myrdal	Sweden
1983	Lech Walesa	Poland

Man Has Created Many Earth Satellites

Satellite	Country	Year Launched	Importance
Sputnik 1	U.S.S.R.	1957	First satellite launched
Vanguard 1	U.S.	1958	First to study Earth from orbit, revealed its "pear shape"
Tiros 1	U.S.	1960	Relayed first cloud-cover photos
Echo 1	U.S.	1960	Relayed first voice and television signals
Vostok 1	U.S.S.R.	1961	First manned satellite
OSO-1[1]	U.S.	1962	Studied Sun's effects on Earth
Voskhod 1	U.S.S.R.	1964	Carried first 3-man crew
OGO-1[2]	U.S.	1964	Studied interaction of Earth and Sun
Voskhod 2	U.S.S.R.	1965	First "walk in space"
Nimbus 2	U.S.	1966	Telecast day and night cloud cover, and measured Earth's heat balance
ATS-1[3]	U.S.	1966	Tests in space new techniques and equipment for future use
Explorer 38	U.S.	1968	Huge antennas study radio waves from distant parts of our galaxy
OAO-2[4]	U.S.	1968	Outside Earth's atmosphere its 11 telescopes study the stars
Soyuz 4- Soyuz 5	U.S.S.R.	1969	First space transfer between crafts
NATOSAT-1	U.S.	1970	Carries military communications
Salyut 1	U.S.S.R.	1971	First orbiting space station
ERTS-1[5]	U.S.	1972	Reports air and water pollution, forest and crop conditions, ice movements and ocean currents
Skylab	U.S.	1973	Orbital laboratory manned by 3 crews of 3 men for a total of 171 days
Soyuz 35	U.S.S.R.	1980	Record endurance 185 days

[1] Orbiting Solar Observatory   [3] Applications Technology Satellite   [5] Earth Resources Technology
[2] Orbiting Geophysical Observatory   [4] Orbiting Astronomical Observatory   Satellite

Man Has Explored the Solar System

Probe	Country	Year Launched	Importance
Pioneer 1	U.S.	1958	First moon shot
Luna 1	U.S.S.R.	1959	First probe to hit the moon
Pioneer 5	U.S.	1960	Transmitted radio signals from space for 2½ months after launch
Mariner 2	U.S.	1962	First successful flight past Venus
Ranger 7	U.S.	1964	Relayed surface photos for 15 minutes before impact on the moon
Mariner 4	U.S.	1964	Returned first photos of Mars
Venus 3	U.S.S.R.	1965	First probe to land on a planet
Lunar Orbiter 1	U.S.	1966	Explored moon and its environment
Luna 9	U.S.S.R.	1966	First soft landing on the moon
Apollo 9	U.S.	1969	Simulated, in Earth orbit, landing of lunar module, return to and docking with command module
Apollo 11	U.S.	1969	First men land on the Moon
Apollo 15	U.S.	1971	First travel on Moon in Lunar Roving Vehicle, first deep-space walk
Mariner 9	U.S.	1971	Entered Mars orbit and returned 7,000 photos of planet's surface
Mars 3	U.S.S.R.	1971	Soft landed space robot on Mars
Pioneer 10	U.S.	1972	Near perfect launch of probe to study Jupiter and the outer fringes of our solar system
Venus 8	U.S.S.R.	1972	Soft landed on Venus, returned data on solar radiation and the hydrogen halo around Venus
Apollo 17	U.S.	1972	Most successful moon probe, last in the Apollo program
Columbia	U.S.	1983	Space-shuttle six-man flight

222

Numbers Tell Us
Many Things

NUMBERS ARE A LANGUAGE all to themselves. They describe to us how long something is, how heavy it is, how much space it takes up, and how much it costs. Numbers are important in everyone's daily life, whether they describe the 3 pennies left over from someone's allowance or that the sun is 93,000,000 miles away from the earth.

Listed here are the measurements used in the United States (English system), those used in many different countries (Metric system), and the different ways to measure temperature. There are also lists of the values of money in the United States and in other countries.

Numerals

The most common numerals used throughout the world are the ones we see everyday. They are called *Hindu-Arabic*.

1 2 3 4 5 6 7 8 9 0

Other numerals that are used occasionally are **Roman numerals**.

I	II	III	IV	V	VI	VII	VIII	IX	X	L	C	D	M
1	**2**	**3**	**4**	**5**	**6**	**7**	**8**	**9**	**10**	**50**	**100**	**500**	**1,000**

There have been other sets of numerals used throughout history.

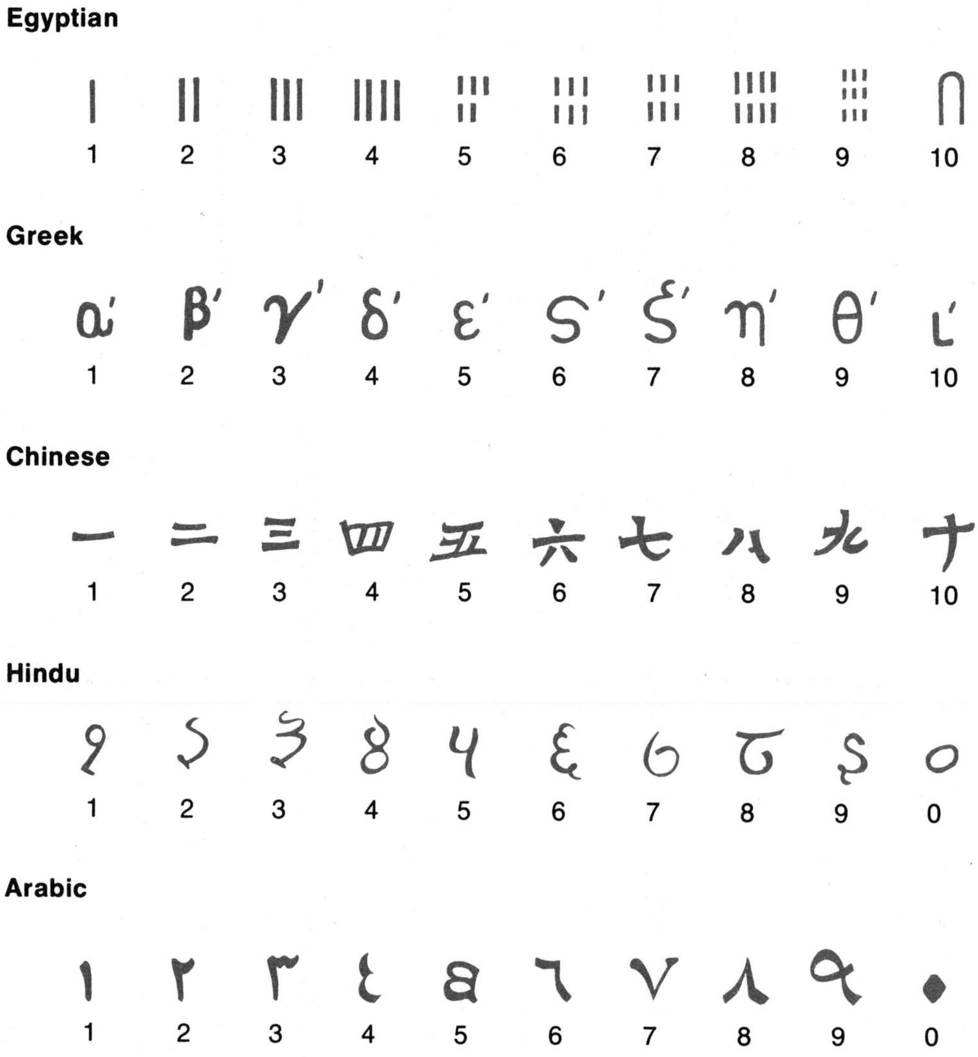

Egyptian

| 1 | 2 | 3 | 4 | 5 | 6 | 7 | 8 | 9 | 10 |

Greek

| 1 | 2 | 3 | 4 | 5 | 6 | 7 | 8 | 9 | 10 |

Chinese

| 1 | 2 | 3 | 4 | 5 | 6 | 7 | 8 | 9 | 10 |

Hindu

| 1 | 2 | 3 | 4 | 5 | 6 | 7 | 8 | 9 | 0 |

Arabic

| 1 | 2 | 3 | 4 | 5 | 6 | 7 | 8 | 9 | 0 |

Temperature Scale

Temperatures

There are two measures of temperature—*Fahrenheit* and *Celsius*. Fahrenheit is the measure most commonly used in the United States and England. The Celsius scale is used in many other parts of the world, and its use is becoming more widespread in the United States.

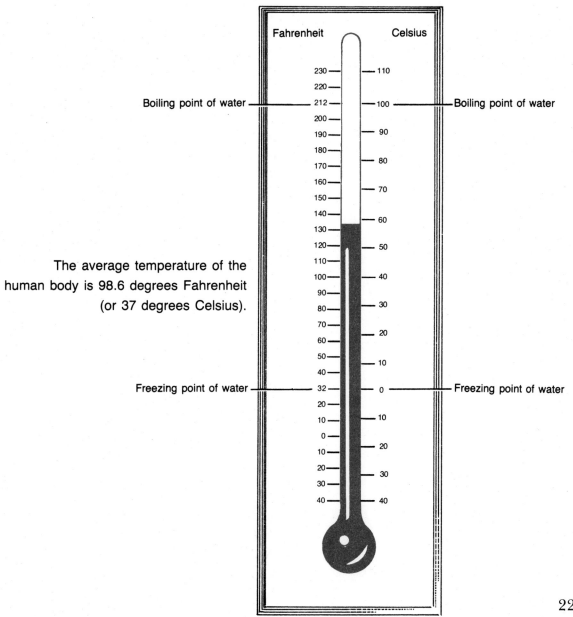

Boiling point of water — 212 · · · 100 — Boiling point of water

The average temperature of the human body is 98.6 degrees Fahrenheit (or 37 degrees Celsius).

Freezing point of water — 32 · · · 0 — Freezing point of water

Weights and Measures

Length

English System	Equals	Equals in Metric System
Inch	------	25.4 millimeters
Foot	12 inches	.3048 meter
Yard	3 feet	.9144 meter
Rod	5½ yards	5.0292 meters
Furlong	40 rods	201.1684 meters
Mile	8 furlongs	1.6093 kilometers

Metric System	Equals	Equals in English System
Millimeter	------	.0394 inch
Centimeter	10 millimeters	.3937 inch
Decimeter	10 centimeters	3.937 inches
Meter	10 decimeters	1.0936 yards
Kilometer	1,000 meters	.62137 mile

Area

English System	Equals	Equals in Metric System
Square Inch	------	6.4516 square centimeters
Square Foot	144 square inches	.0929 square meter
Square Yard	9 square feet	.8361 square meter
Square Rod	30¼ square yards	25.293 square meters
Acre	160 square rods	.4047 hectare
Square Mile	640 acres	2.59 square kilometers

Metric System	Equals	Equals in English System
Square Millimeter	------	.0015 square inch
Square Centimeter	100 sq. millimeters	.155 square inch
Square Decimeter	100 sq. centimeters	15.5 square inches
Square Meter	100 sq. decimeters	10.7639 square feet
Are	100 sq. meters	3.9537 square rods
Hectare	100 ares	2.471 acres
Square Kilometer	100 hectares	.3861 square mile

Weights and Measures

Weight

English System (Avoirdupois)	Equals	Equals in Metric System
Grain	------	.0648 gram
Dram	27.3438 grains	1.7718 grams
Ounce	16 drams	28.3495 grams
Pound	16 ounces	.4536 kilogram
Ton	2,000 pounds	.9072 metric ton

(Besides the *Avoirdupois* measure of weights in the English System, there are also two different measures—*Troy* and *Apothecaries*. Troy weight is used for weighing gold and silver, and Apothecaries' weight is for measuring medical prescriptions.

Metric System	Equals	Equals in English System (Avoirdupois)
Milligram	------	.0154 grain
Centigram	10 milligrams	.1543 grain
Decigram	10 centigrams	1.5432 grains
Gram	10 decigrams	.0353 ounce
Kilogram	1,000 grams	2.2046 pounds
Metric Ton	1,000 kilograms	1.1023 tons

Capacity

(In the United States there are both *liquid* and *dry* measures. In the metric system, there is only one measure for both liquid and dry units.)

United States—Liquid Measure

	Equals	Equals in Metric System
Fluid Ounce	------	29.5729 milliliters
Pint	16 fluid ounces	.4732 liter
Quart	2 pints	.9463 liter
Gallon	4 quarts	3.7853 liters

United States—Dry Measure

	Equals	Equals in Metric System
Pint	------	.5506 liter
Quart	2 pints	1.1012 liters
Peck	8 quarts	8.8096 liters
Bushel	4 pecks	35.2383 liters

Metric System

	Equals	Equal to U.S. Liquid Measure	Equal to U.S. Dry Measure
Milliliter	------	.0338 fluid ounce	.0018 pint
Centiliter	10 milliliters	.3381 fluid ounce	.0182 pint
Deciliter	10 centiliters	3.3815 fluid ounces	.1816 pint
Liter	10 deciliters	1.0567 quarts	.9081 quart

Volume

English System	Equals	Equals in Metric System
Cubic Inch	------	16.3872 cubic centimeters
Cubic Foot	1728 cubic inches	.0283 cubic meter
Cubic Yard	27 cubic feet	.7646 cubic meter
Cord	128 cubic feet	3.6246 cubic meters

Metric System	Equals	Equals in English System
Cubic Millimeter	------	.00006 cubic inch
Cubic Centimeter	1,000 cubic millimeters	.061 cubic inch
Cubic Decimeter	1,000 cubic centimeters	61.0234 cubic inches
Cubic Meter (Stere)	1,000 cubic decimeters	35.3145 cubic feet

Coins and Currency
in the United States

★ ★ ★ ★ ★

Coins

Denomination		Portrait on Coin
Cent (Penny)	$ .01	Abraham Lincoln
Nickel	.05	Thomas Jefferson
Dime	.10	Franklin D. Roosevelt
Quarter	.25	George Washington
Half-dollar	.50	John F. Kennedy
Dollar	1.00	Dwight D. Eisenhower

★ ★ ★ ★ ★

Currency (Paper Money or "bills")

Denomination	Portrait on Bill
$ 1.	George Washington
$ 2.	Thomas Jefferson
$ 5.	Abraham Lincoln
$ 10.	Alexander Hamilton
$ 20.	Andrew Jackson
$ 50.	Ulysses S. Grant
$ 100.	Benjamin Franklin
$ 500.	William McKinley
$ 1,000.	Grover Cleveland
$ 5,000.	James Madison
$ 10,000.	Salmon P. Chase
$100,000.	Woodrow Wilson

Money from Different Countries

Country	Monetary Unit
Australia	Dollar
Belgium	Franc
Brazil	Cruzeiro
Canada	Dollar
China	
People's Republic	Yuan
China	
Nationalist (Taiwan)	Dollar
Denmark	Krone
Egypt	Pound
England	Pound
France	Franc
Germany (West)	Deutsche Mark
Greece	Drachma
Haiti	Gourde
India	Rupee
Ireland	Pound
Israel	Shekel
Italy	Lira
Japan	Yen
Korea	Hwan
Mexico	Peso
Netherlands	Guilder
Pakistan	Rupee
Portugal	Escudo
Saudi Arabia	Riyal
Spain	Peseta
Sweden	Krona
Turkey	Lira
U.S.S.R.	Ruble
Vietnam (South)	Piastre
Yugoslavia	Dinar

Our United States

THE EXCITING STORY of the United States began with the Indians, our first citizens. The Indians lived with and sometimes fought with the people who came from Europe to settle in America. In the early days, it was a small nation, only 13 colonies. The people wanted to be free, and they fought until their freedom was won.

The country grew to have 50 states, each separate but all united. Contained in this section are facts about the Indians, the colonies and Civil War states, signers of the Declaration of Independence, our presidents, the 50 states, and the U.S. government today.

The Indians—The First Americans

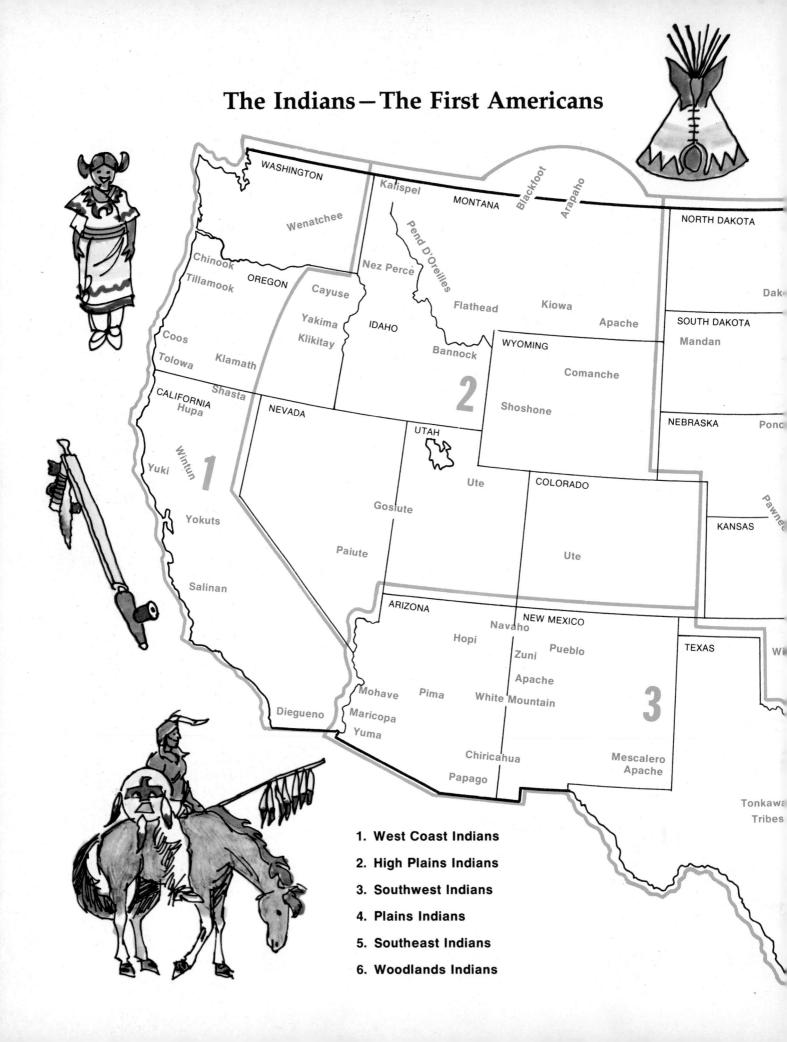

WASHINGTON

Kalispel

MONTANA

Blackfoot

Arapaho

NORTH DAKOTA

Wenatchee

Chinook

Pend D'Oreilles

Tillamook

OREGON

Nez Percé

Cayuse

Flathead

Kiowa

Dak

Yakima

IDAHO

Apache

SOUTH DAKOTA

Coos

Klikitay

Mandan

Tolowa

Klamath

Bannock

WYOMING

Shasta

NEVADA

Comanche

CALIFORNIA

Hupa

Shoshone

NEBRASKA

Ponc

Yuki

Wintun

1

UTAH

COLORADO

Yokuts

Ute

Pawnee

Goslute

KANSAS

Paiute

Ute

Salinan

ARIZONA

NEW MEXICO

Navaho

Mohave

Hopi

Pueblo

TEXAS

Wi

Zuni

Diegueno

Maricopa

Pima

Apache

3

Yuma

White Mountain

Chiricahua

Mescalero
Apache

Papago

Tonkawa
Tribes

2

1. **West Coast Indians**

2. **High Plains Indians**

3. **Southwest Indians**

4. **Plains Indians**

5. **Southeast Indians**

6. **Woodlands Indians**

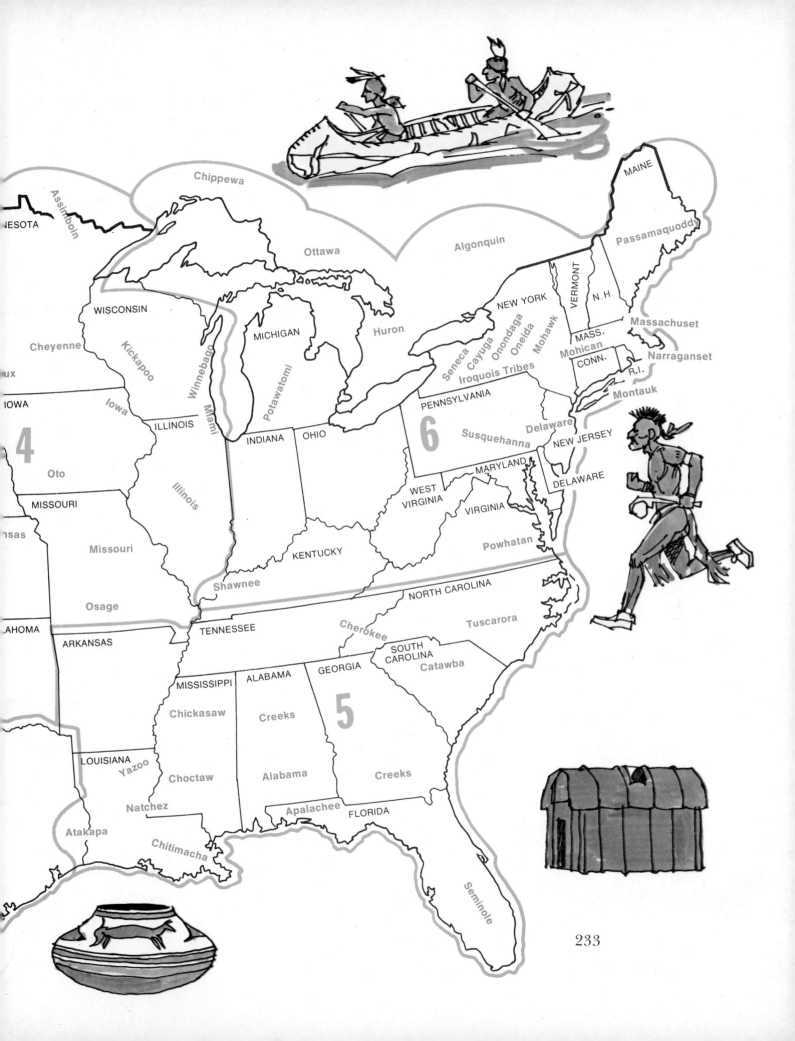

NESOTA

Assiniboin

Chippewa

MINNESOTA

Ottawa

Algonquin

MAINE

Passamaquoddy

WISCONSIN

Cheyenne

Kickapoo

MICHIGAN

Huron

VERMONT

NEW YORK

N.H.

Winnebago

Seneca

Onondaga

Cayuga

Oneida

Mohawk

Iroquois Tribes

MASS.

Mohican

CONN.

Massachuset

Narraganset

Oto

Iowa

Iowa

ILLINOIS

Potawatomi

Miami

INDIANA

OHIO

PENNSYLVANIA

6

Susquehanna

Delaware

R.I.

Montauk

NEW JERSEY

DELAWARE

Delaware

4

MISSOURI

Illinois

MARYLAND

WEST
VIRGINIA

VIRGINIA

nsas

Missouri

KENTUCKY

Powhatan

Osage

Shawnee

NORTH CAROLINA

AHOMA

ARKANSAS

TENNESSEE

Cherokee

Tuscarora

SOUTH
CAROLINA

Catawba

MISSISSIPPI

ALABAMA

GEORGIA

Chickasaw

Creeks

5

LOUISIANA

Yazoo

Choctaw

Alabama

Creeks

Natchez

Apalachee

FLORIDA

Atakapa

Chitimacha

Seminole

233

The Men Who Signed Our Declaration of Independence

Signer	State	Signer	State
John Adams	Massachusetts	Thomas Lynch Jr.	South Carolina
Samuel Adams	Massachusetts	Thomas McKean	Delaware
Josiah Bartlett	New Hampshire	Arthur Middleton	South Carolina
Carter Braxton	Virginia	Lewis Morris	New York
Charles Carroll	Maryland	Robert Morris	Pennsylvania
Samuel Chase	Maryland	John Morton	Pennsylvania
Abram Clark	New Jersey	Thomas Nelson Jr.	Virginia
George Clymer	Pennsylvania	William Paca	Maryland
William Ellery	Rhode Island	Robert Treat Paine	Massachusetts
William Floyd	New York	John Penn	North Carolina
Benjamin Franklin	Pennsylvania	George Read	Delaware
Elbridge Gerry	Massachusetts	Caesar Rodney	Delaware
Button Gwinnett	Georgia	George Ross	Pennsylvania
Lyman Hall	Georgia	Benjamin Rush	Pennsylvania
John Hancock	Massachusetts	Edward Rutledge	South Carolina
Benjamin Harrison	Virginia	Roger Sherman	Connecticut
John Hart	New Jersey	James Smith	Pennsylvania
Joseph Hewes	North Carolina	Richard Stockton	New Jersey
Thomas Heyward Jr.	South Carolina	Thomas Stone	Maryland
William Hooper	North Carolina	George Taylor	Pennsylvania
Stephen Hopkins	Rhode Island	Matthew Thornton	New Hampshire
Francis Hopkinson	New Jersey	George Walton	Georgia
Samuel Huntington	Connecticut	William Whipple	New Hampshire
Thomas Jefferson	Virginia	William Williams	Connecticut
Richard Henry Lee	Virginia	James Wilson	Pennsylvania
Francis Lightfoot Lee	Virginia	John Witherspoon	New Jersey
Francis Lewis	New York	Oliver Wolcott	Connecticut
Philip Livingston	New York	George Wythe	Virginia

234

The Original Thirteen Colonies

Colony	First Permanent Settlement	Entered Union
Connecticut	Hartford (1635)	Jan. 9, 1788
Delaware	Wilmington (1638)	Dec. 7, 1787
Georgia	Savannah (1733)	Jan. 2, 1788
Maryland	St. Mary's (1634)	Apr. 28, 1788
Massachusetts	Plymouth (1620)	Feb. 6, 1788
New Hampshire	Rye (1623)	June 21, 1788
New Jersey	Elizabeth (1664)	Dec. 18, 1787
New York	New York City (1614)	July 26, 1788
North Carolina	Albemarle (1653)	Nov. 21, 1789
Pennsylvania	Tinicum Island (1643)	Dec. 12, 1787
Rhode Island	Providence (1636)	May 29, 1790
South Carolina	Albemarle Point (1670)	May 23, 1788
Virginia	Jamestown (1607)	June 25, 1788

The Civil War States (1861-1865)

Union		Confederacy	Date of Secession
California	Minnesota	Alabama	January 11, 1861
Connecticut	Missouri	Arkansas	May 6, 1861
Delaware	Nevada	Florida	January 10, 1861
Illinois	New Hampshire	Georgia	January 19, 1861
Indiana	New Jersey	Louisiana	January 26, 1861
Iowa	New York	Mississippi	January 9, 1861
Kansas	Ohio	North Carolina	May 20, 1861
Kentucky	Oregon	South Carolina	December 20, 1860
Maine	Pennsylvania	Tennessee	June 8, 1861
Maryland	Rhode Island	Texas	March 2, 1861
Massachusetts	Vermont	Virginia	April 17, 1861
Michigan	West Virginia		
Wisconsin			

Presidents of  the United States

President	State	Political Party	Occupation	Term of Office
George Washington	Virginia	Federalist	Planter, Soldier	1789-1797
John Adams	Massachusetts	Federalist	Lawyer	1797-1801
Thomas Jefferson	Virginia	Democratic Republican	Lawyer	1801-1809
James Madison	Virginia	Democratic Republican	Planter	1809-1817
James Monroe	Virginia	Democratic Republican	Lawyer	1817-1825
John Quincy Adams	Massachusetts	Democratic Republican	Lawyer	1825-1829
Andrew Jackson	South Carolina	Democrat	Lawyer, Soldier	1829-1837
Martin Van Buren	New York	Democrat	Lawyer	1837-1841
William H. Harrison	Virginia	Whig	Soldier	1841
John Tyler	Virginia	Whig	Lawyer	1841-1845
James K. Polk	North Carolina	Democrat	Lawyer	1845-1849
Zachary Taylor	Virginia	Whig	Soldier	1849-1850
Millard Fillmore	New York	Whig	Lawyer	1850-1853
Franklin Pierce	New Hampshire	Democrat	Lawyer	1853-1857
James Buchanan	Pennsylvania	Democrat	Lawyer	1857-1861
Abraham Lincoln	Kentucky	Republican	Lawyer	1861-1865
Andrew Johnson	North Carolina	Democrat	Legislator	1865-1869
Ulysses S. Grant	Ohio	Republican	Soldier	1869-1877
Rutherford B. Hayes	Ohio	Republican	Lawyer	1877-1881
James A. Garfield	Ohio	Republican	Educator, Soldier	1881

Presidents of  the United States

President	State	Political Party	Occupation	Term of Office
Chester A. Arthur	Vermont	Republican	Lawyer	1881-1885
Grover Cleveland	New Jersey	Democrat	Lawyer	1885-1889
Benjamin Harrison	Ohio	Republican	Lawyer	1889-1893
Grover Cleveland	New Jersey	Democrat	Lawyer	1893-1897
William McKinley	Ohio	Republican	Lawyer, Soldier	1897-1901
Theodore Roosevelt	New York	Republican	Soldier	1901-1909
William Howard Taft	Ohio	Republican	Lawyer	1909-1913
Woodrow Wilson	Virginia	Democrat	Educator, Lawyer	1913-1921
Warren G. Harding	Ohio	Republican	Newspaper Publisher	1921-1923
Calvin Coolidge	Vermont	Republican	Lawyer	1923-1929
Herbert C. Hoover	Iowa	Republican	Mining Engineer	1929-1933
Franklin D. Roosevelt	New York	Democrat	Lawyer	1933-1945
Harry S. Truman	Missouri	Democrat	Businessman, Legislator	1945-1953
Dwight D. Eisenhower	Texas	Republican	Soldier	1953-1961
John F. Kennedy	Massachusetts	Democrat	Legislator	1961-1963
Lyndon B. Johnson	Texas	Democrat	Legislator	1963-1968
Richard M. Nixon	California	Republican	Lawyer	1969-1974
Gerald R. Ford	Michigan	Republican	Lawyer	1974-1977
James Earl Carter	Georgia	Democrat	Businessman	1977-1981
Ronald Reagan	California	Republican	Actor	1981-

The Fifty States

State	Capital	Entered Union	Reps. in Cong.	Flower	Bird
Alabama	Montgomery	1819	7	Camellia	Yellowhammer
Alaska	Juneau	1959	1	Forget-me-not	Willow Ptarmigan
Arizona	Phoenix	1912	4	Saguaro	Cactus Wren
Arkansas	Little Rock	1836	4	Apple blossom	Mockingbird
California	Sacramento	1850	43	Golden poppy	California Valley Quail
Colorado	Denver	1876	5	Rocky Mountain columbine	Lark Bunting
Connecticut	Hartford	1788	7	Mountain laurel	Robin
Delaware	Dover	1787	1	Peach blossom	Blue Hen Chicken
Florida	Tallahassee	1845	15	Orange blossom	Mockingbird
Georgia	Atlanta	1788	10	Cherokee rose	Brown Thresher
Hawaii	Honolulu	1959	2	Red hibiscus	Hawaiian Goose
Idaho	Boise	1890	2	Syringa	Mountain Bluebird
Illinois	Springfield	1818	24	Violet	Cardinal
Indiana	Indianapolis	1816	11	Peony	Cardinal
Iowa	Des Moines	1846	6	Wild rose	Eastern Goldfinch
Kansas	Topeka	1861	5	Sunflower	Western Meadow Lark
Kentucky	Frankfort	1792	7	Goldenrod	Cardinal
Louisiana	Baton Rouge	1812	8	Magnolia	Eastern Brown Pelican
Maine	Augusta	1820	2	White pine cone and tassel	Chickadee
Maryland	Annapolis	1788	8	Blackeyed Susan	Baltimore Oriole
Massachusetts	Boston	1788	12	Mayflower	Chickadee
Michigan	Lansing	1837	19	Apple blossom	Robin
Minnesota	St. Paul	1858	8	Showy lady's slipper	Common Loon
Mississippi	Jackson	1817	5	Magnolia	Mockingbird
Missouri	Jefferson City	1821	10	Hawthorn	Bluebird

Nickname	Motto
Yellowhammer State	We dare defend our rights
Land of the Midnight Sun	North to the future
Grand Canyon State	God enriches
Land of Opportunity	The people rule
Golden State	Eureka (I have found it)
Centennial State	Nothing without providence
Nutmeg State	He who transplanted still sustains
Diamond State	Liberty and independence
Sunshine State	In God we trust
Peach State	Wisdom, justice and moderation
Aloha State	The life of the land is perpetuated in righteousness
Gem State	May you last forever
Prairie State	State sovereignty, national union
Hoosier State	The crossroads of America
Hawkeye State	Our liberties we prize and our rights we will maintain
Sunflower State	To the stars through difficulties
Bluegrass State	United we stand, divided we fall
Pelican State	Union, justice and confidence
Pine Tree State	I guide
Free State	Deeds are masculine, words are feminine
Bay State	By the sword we seek peace, but peace only under liberty
Wolverine State	If you seek a pleasant peninsula, look about you
Gopher State	The star of the north
Magnolia State	By valor and arms
The Show-Me State	The welfare of the people shall be the supreme law

The Fifty States

State	Capital	Entered Union	Reps. in Cong.	Flower	Bird
Montana	Helena	1889	2	Bitter root	Western Meadow Lark
Nebraska	Lincoln	1867	3	Goldenrod	Western Meadow Lark
Nevada	Carson City	1864	1	Sagebrush	Mountain Bluebird
New Hampshire	Concord	1788	2	Purple lilac	Purple Finch
New Jersey	Trenton	1787	15	Violet	Eastern Goldfinch
New Mexico	Santa Fe	1912	2	Yucca	Road Runner
New York	Albany	1788	41	Rose	Bluebird
North Carolina	Raleigh	1789	11	Dogwood	Cardinal
North Dakota	Bismarck	1889	2	Wild prairie rose	Western Meadow Lark
Ohio	Columbus	1803	24	Scarlet carnation	Cardinal
Oklahoma	Oklahoma City	1907	6	Mistletoe	Scissor-Tailed Flycatcher
Oregon	Salem	1859	4	Oregon grape	Western Meadow Lark
Pennsylvania	Harrisburg	1787	27	Mountain laurel	Ruffed Grouse
Rhode Island	Providence	1790	2	Violet	Rhode Island Red
South Carolina	Columbia	1788	6	Carolina jasmine	Carolina Wren
South Dakota	Pierre	1889	2	Pasqueflower	Ring-Necked Pheasant
Tennessee	Nashville	1796	9	Iris	Mockingbird
Texas	Austin	1845	23	Bluebonnet	Mockingbird
Utah	Salt Lake City	1896	2	Sego lily	Seagull
Vermont	Montpelier	1791	1	Red clover	Hermit Thrush
Virginia	Richmond	1788	10	Dogwood	Cardinal
Washington	Olympia	1889	7	Coast rhododendron	Willow Goldfinch
West Virginia	Charleston	1863	5	Rhododendron	Cardinal
Wisconsin	Madison	1848	10	Violet	Robin
Wyoming	Cheyenne	1890	1	Indian paintbrush	Meadow Lark

Nickname	Motto
Treasure State	Gold and silver
Cornhusker State	Equality before the law
Sagebrush State	All for our country
Granite State	Live free or die
Garden State	Liberty and prosperity
Land of Enchantment	It grows as it goes
Empire State	Ever upward
Tar Heel State	To be rather than to seem
Sioux State	Liberty and union, now and forever, one and inseparable
Buckeye State	With God, all things are possible
Sooner State	Labor conquers all things
Beaver State	The Union
Keystone State	Virtue, liberty, and independence
Little Rhody	Hope
Palmetto State	Prepared in mind and resources
Sunshine State	Under God the people rule
Volunteer State	Tennessee—America at its best
Lone Star State	Friendship
Beehive State	Industry
Green Mountain State	Vermont— freedom and unity
Old Dominion State	Thus always to tyrants
Evergreen State	Bye and bye
Mountain State	Mountaineers are always free
Badger State	Forward
Equality State	Equal rights

The United States Government Today

Executive Branch

President
Vice President

Cabinet Departments

State	Agriculture	Health and Human Services
Treasury	Commerce	Transportation
Defense	Labor	Housing and Urban Development
Justice	Energy	Education
Interior		

Important Bureaus and Offices in The Executive Branch

	Division of
Air Force	Defense
Alcohol, Drug Abuse, and Mental Health	Health and Human Services
Army	Defense
Bureau of Alcohol, Tobacco, and Firearms	Treasury
Census	Commerce
Centers for Disease Control	Health and Human Services
Coast Guard	Transportation
Council of Economic Advisers	Executive Office
Customs	Treasury
Defense Intelligence Agency	Defense
Drug Enforcement Administration	Justice
Federal Bureau of Investigation	Justice
Fish and Wildlife Service	Interior
Food and Drug Administration	Health and Human Services
Food and Nutrition Service	Agriculture
Foreign Service	State
Forest Service	Agriculture
Geological Survey	Interior
Health Care Financing Administration	Health and Human Services

	Division of
Immigration and Naturalization Service	Justice
Indian Affairs	Interior
Internal Revenue Service	Treasury
Labor Statistics	Labor
Land Management	Interior
Marine Corps	Defense
Mine Safety and Health Administration	Labor
Mines, Bureau of	Interior
National Bureau of Standards	Commerce
National Institutes of Health	Health and Human Services
National Oceanic and Atmospheric Administration	Commerce
National Parks Service	Interior
National Security Council	Executive Office
Navy	Defense
Office of Management and Budget	Executive Office
Patent and Trademark Office	Commerce
Secret Service	Treasury
Social Security Administration	Health and Human Services
Soil Conservation Service	Agriculture

The United States Government Today

Legislative Branch

House of Representatives

Speaker of the House

435 members
The number from each state is determined by the population of the state. (See *THE FIFTY STATES* for number from each state.)

Senate

President of the Senate
(Vice-President of the U.S.)

100 members
2 from each state

★ ★ ★

Judicial Branch

Supreme Court
(Chief Justice and 8 associate justices)

Court of Appeals

District Courts

Special Courts

Court of Claims   Territorial Courts
Court of Military Appeals   Customs Court
Court of Customs and Patent Appeals

Independent Agencies in The Executive Branch

ACTION
Agency for International Development
Arms Control and Disarmament Agency
Central Intelligence Agency
Consumer Product Safety Commission
Environmental Protection Agency
Equal Employment Opportunity Commission
Federal Communications Commission
Federal Deposit Insurance Corporation
Federal Election Commission
Federal Home Loan Bank Board
Federal Mediation and Conciliation Service
Federal Reserve System
Federal Trade Commission
General Services Administration
International Communications Agency

Interstate Commerce Commission
National Aeronautics and Space Administration
National Endowment for the Arts
National Endowment for the Humanities
National Labor Relations Board
National Mediation Board
National Science Foundation
Nuclear Regulatory Commission
Securities and Exchange Commission
Selective Service System
Small Business Administration
Smithsonian Institution
Tennessee Valley Authority
United States Postal Service
Veterans Administration

Sports

SPORTS ARE FUN TO WATCH, and it is exciting to cheer for favorite teams and athletes. But, most of all, sports are fun to play. Baseball, football, and basketball are probably the 3 most popular sports in America, for both the athletes and their fans. Other favorite sports include swimming, skiing, track and field events, tennis, golf, soccer, and volleyball.

Each sport has its own set of rules and equipment, but there is one ideal common to all sports: "It is not whether you win or lose, but how you play the game." Keep this in mind as you play, and you should always enjoy your favorite sports.

⑧

⑦ ⑨

⑥ ④

⑤ ① ③

②

Playing positions are as follows:
1. Pitcher
2. Catcher
3. First Baseman
4. Second Baseman
5. Third Baseman
6. Shortstop
7. Left Fielder
8. Center Fielder
9. Right Fielder

In baseball (9-inch), the bases are placed 90 feet apart.

In softball (12-inch), the bases are 60 feet apart; in 16-inch softball the bases are only 45 feet apart.

Baseball

The object of the game is to see which team can score more runs during the innings the teams have agreed to play. A team scores a run when a player, after reaching first, second, and third base, safely crosses home plate.

In order to start a baseball game, you should have the following:

1. **Playing area**—An outdoor area on which a diamond can be laid out (see diagram).
2. **Bases**—Pieces of cardboard or something else to use as bases.
3. **Bat and ball**—The ball may be a regulation league baseball (9-inch), or a rubber ball the same size. Softball is played with a larger ball (either 12-inch or 16-inch). The playing area for softball is smaller (see diagram this page). A plain rubber ball is suggested for boys just learning to play baseball.
4. **Gloves**—When playing with a ball the size of a regulation league baseball or a 12-inch softball, all players in the field should wear gloves. Gloves are not necessary if you are playing with a 16-inch softball.
5. **Players**—Enough boys for two teams. A full team has nine players. "Choose-up" games can be played with as few as five players on a team (see diagram).

Players should understand the following base-ball terms:

1. **Inning**—The period of time when both teams bat. Team 1 bats until it makes three outs. Then it takes the field and team 2 comes to bat. When team 2 makes three outs, the inning is over. Games are usually seven or nine innings. Players may decide to play fewer innings if they wish. More innings are played if the score is tied at the end of the game.

2. **Pitch**—The throwing of the ball over home plate by the pitcher of the team in the field. In hardball (9-inch) the pitch is thrown overhand. In softball (12-inch or 16-inch) it is thrown underhand.

3. **Strike**—If the batter does not swing at the ball when it is pitched, and the pitch is over home plate and between the knees and shoulders of the batter, the pitch is called a strike. It is also a strike if the batter swings at a pitched ball and misses. A ball hit into foul territory and not caught on the fly (before touching the ground) by the opposition is also called a strike. A foul ball hit on the *third* strike does not count, and the batter is not out.

4. **Ball**—If a pitched ball is not swung at, and if the ball does not come over home plate, or is over the plate but below the batter's knees or above his shoulders, it is called a ball.

5. **Walk**—The batter is allowed to go to first base if the pitcher throws four balls.

6. **Strike Out**—The batter is out for having three strikes.

7. **Fair Ball**—A batted ball that is hit somewhere between the first and third baselines. The

team in the field must play this ball in order to get the batter out.

8. **Foul Ball** — A batted ball outside either the first or third baselines. The batter is out only if a member of the opposition catches the ball on the fly.

Remember the following when you are at bat:

1. Grip the bat in both hands above the knob at the bottom of the bat. If you are right-handed, your right hand should be above your left hand. The bottom of your right hand touches the top of your left hand.
2. Hold the bat in an upright position with your hands about chest high and away from your body. Do not let the bat rest on your shoulder as the pitcher prepares to pitch the ball.
3. When the pitcher throws the ball, watch the ball all the way until your bat hits it.
4. After hitting the ball, drop the bat. Do not throw it! Run to first base as fast as you can.

The team in the field tries to get each of the opposition batters out. A batter is out if:

1. He strikes out.
2. The batted ball is caught on the fly in fair or foul territory by a member of the opposition.
3. He hits a fair ball on the ground (a grounder), and a player in the field catches the ball and throws it to the first baseman, who tags first base before the batter touches first base. The first baseman only needs to tag first base with his foot. If the ball is hit to the first baseman, a teammate may cover first base.
4. After hitting a fair ball and arriving safely at first, the batter is tagged with the ball by a member of the opposition before he gets to second base, third base, or home plate.

The batter is safe at first base if:

1. He gets a walk.
2. A batted ball in fair territory is not caught on the fly, and the batter reaches first base before a member of the opposition with the ball tags first base.

The batter who has reached first base safely may try for second base if he thinks he can reach it before an opposing team member gets the ball and tags him with the ball. If the batter is tagged before he reaches second base, he is out. The same is true if the batter tries for third base after reaching second base safely, or if he tries to get to home plate after reaching third base safely.

If a player is on first base and the next batter hits any fair ball that is not caught on the fly by the opposition, the base runner must advance to another base. He may only move *forward* (to second base to third base to home plate).

When the base runners advance on a batted ball, the opposition may get an out:

1. If a player in the field gets the ball and tags second base before the runner on first reaches second base. This type of an out is called a "force out."
2. If there are runners on first and second base, then the team in the field can force them out at second or third base. If there are runners on all the bases, there are possible outs at home plate, at third base, and at second base.
3. If a runner is tagged with the ball by a player in the field while the runner is off the base or between bases.

If a batted ball is caught on the fly by the team in the field, the batter is out, and a base runner cannot advance to the next base until after the ball has been caught. If the base runner leaves his base before the ball is caught, and the opposition tags the base the runner left, the base runner is out. Two outs would have been made on one play. This is called a "double play."

A base runner does not have to advance to the next base on a batted ball if he is on second or third base and there is no runner on first base. In this situation, the base runner should stay where he is if he does not think he can get to the next base without being tagged out. Remember, though, that when the ball is batted, base runners should try to advance as far as possible so they can score a run.

A base runner can never pass another base runner in front of him. A runner is out for passing another base runner.

Baseball or softball may be played "pitcher's-hands-out" rather than first-base-out. In pitcher's-hands-out, if a batter hits a grounder to an infielder, the infielder does *not* throw to the first baseman. He throws the ball to the pitcher who must remain in the area of the pitcher's mound. If the pitcher catches the ball before the batter reaches first base, the batter is out.

With young boys, it often makes for a better game if balls and strikes are not called. The only strikes recorded would be foul balls or a swing and a miss. This system encourages boys to swing at the ball and learn to hit. It is also practical because there often is no umpire in a choose-up game.

Since catching equipment (mask, chest protector, shin guards, cup) is usually available only in organized leagues, catchers in choose-up games should stand far behind the batter.

Young boys should also play in gym shoes rather than in spiked "baseball shoes."

Basketball

The object of the game is to put the ball through the basket. This is the only way a team can score points. The team with the most points at the end of the game is the winner.

In order to start a game you must have:

1. **Basketball court**—Gymnasiums have regulation courts with baskets at both ends of the court (see diagram this page). Outdoor courts may have just one basket. Such courts are called half-courts. In a full-court game, each team shoots at a different basket. In a half-court game, both teams try to score at the same basket.
2. **Basketball**—Regulation or smaller size.
3. **Players**—Enough boys for two teams. There should be the same number on each team, and no more than five on each team. However, half-court games can be played with as few as two on a team.

All boys interested in basketball should develop the following skills:

1. **Shooting**—Every boy should learn to make shots close to the basket. These shots are called lay-ups. A beginner (right-handed) can learn to shoot a lay-up as follows (a left-

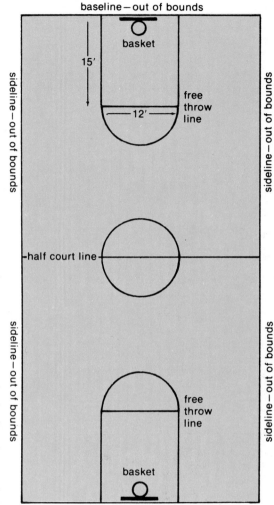

Distances *(fixed)*

Basket to free throw line—15′
Free throw line—12′ wide

Distances *(these can change)*

Sideline to sideline—generally about 40′
Basket to basket—generally at least 80′

251

hander will use the opposite hand and foot):

   a. With the basketball in both hands, you should stand two yards from the basket at an angle of 45 degrees to the backboard. Your feet should be parallel.

   b. Take one full step forward with left foot.

   c. As the left foot hits the ground, jump into the air with the right knee lifted high, and the left leg and ankle extended behind. The ball should be held high above the right shoulder.

   d. At the peak of the jump, thrust the arms upward and push the ball with the right hand, aiming the ball above and to the right of the rim. The ball should bounce off the backboard and into the basket.

   e. After mastering the one-step lay-up, move back 15 feet from the basket. Have someone pass the ball to you as you run towards the basket and shoot a lay-up after catching the pass. Be sure to jump off the left foot, raising the right knee into the air. You should also practice dribbling the ball to the basket for a lay-up.

2. **Passing**—Passing the ball is throwing it from one player to another. Because of the large size of the basketball, pass the ball with *two* hands. Both hands should be securely on the ball. As you pass, a step should be taken in the direction of the teammate you are passing to.

3. **Dribbling**—A player can advance the ball by bouncing it with either his right or left hand; this is dribbling the ball. You may only dribble with one hand at a time. Because it is easier to control the ball with your fingers, the ball should be bounced with your finger-

tips. To advance a ball, a player must dribble it. He cannot run with the ball under his arm. When a player stops dribbling he must:

a. pass the ball to a teammate;

b. shoot the ball at the basket.

4. **Jumping**—This is a vital skill in basketball. You must jump when you shoot a lay-up. You must also jump to get rebounds (missed shots that bounce off the rim of the basket or the backboard).

5. **Defense**—When a team does not have the ball and is trying to stop the other team from scoring, it is said to be on *defense*. Since teams always have the same number of players, it is best to have each player on your team guard a player on the other team. When playing defense, *stay between your assigned man and the basket*. When he has the ball, do not let him dribble to the basket. Try to keep him from catching passes from his teammates.

Basketball is a fast-moving game. One minute your team may have the ball and be trying to score. An instant later you may be on defense because your team has lost the ball. Your team can lose the ball to the other team in the following ways:

1. The opposition may intercept a pass or steal the ball from someone dribbling.

2. The ball may be awarded by the referee to the opposition, who then pass it in from out of bounds, as in the following situations—

   a. If the ball goes out of bounds and a player from your team touched it last, the ball is given to the opposition.

   b. If you or a teammate double-dribble when you have the ball. To double-dribble is to stop dribbling and then start again before passing to a teammate or taking a shot. It is also double-dribbling if you dribble with both hands at the same time.

c. If you or a teammate *travel* (run) with the ball without dribbling.

If you and a member of the opposite team are struggling for the ball at the same time, or if it cannot be determined who has knocked the ball out of bounds, a *jump ball* is called. The ball is thrown up between the two players and they jump to tap it to a teammate.

Players on both teams should avoid body contact. To *foul* an opposing player is to interfere with his action (shooting, passing, catching, dribbling, or playing defense) by body contact such as bumping him, tripping him, grabbing and holding him, or pushing him. When you foul a player, he gets a *free* shot (called *free throw*) at the basket. If you foul him while he is trying to shoot at the basket, he gets two free throws.

The free throw line is 15 feet from the basket. It is marked on all regulation courts. There is a free throw line at both baskets. While the fouled player is shooting his free throw, members of both teams line up beside the free throw line in order to get the rebound if the free throw shooter misses the shot.

Scoring

1. A basket made during actual play is called a field goal and is worth two points.
2. A free throw is worth one point.

When a team scores a basket or a free throw, the ball is given to the opposition, who put the ball in play by passing it in from out of bounds behind the basket.

In organized basketball, a game is divided into four periods or quarters. In elementary school basketball each quarter is six minutes. The team with the highest number of points at the end of four quarters is the winner. If the game ends in a tie, an extra period is played. This is called an overtime period.

Choose-up games, especially on outdoor courts, are very popular with boys. These games are usually half-court games—both teams try to score at the same basket. There are no referees in these games, so the boys playing must be honest in admitting if they have double-dribbled, traveled, fouled, or if they have touched the ball last before it went out of bounds.

When the ball changes hands in a half-court game, the team that has gotten the ball must take it back out past the free throw line before they can try to shoot at the basket. If someone is fouled, he does not shoot a free throw; rather, he passes the ball in bounds for his team so they can try to make a field goal. There are no jump-balls in a half-court game. When a jump-ball situation occurs, the ball is simply awarded to one team who throws it in from out of bounds. The next time the opposite team is given the ball.

The winner of a half-court game is determined by setting a certain number of points as the end of the game. The first team to reach that number of points is the winner.

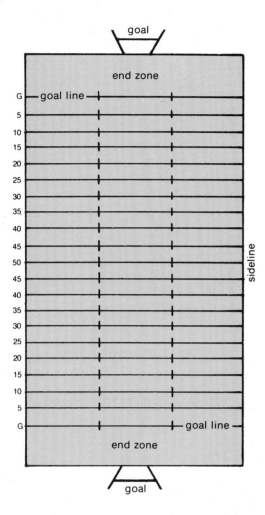

Distances *(for a regulation field)*
Goal line to goal line—100 yards
Goal line to goal post—10 yards
Sideline to sideline—53⅓ yards (160′)
Goal post—at least 20′ high, 18½′ wide
 with a cross bar 10′ high

Football

The object of the game is to advance the football across your opponent's goal line and to prevent him from crossing your goal line.

In order to start a game, you must have:

1. **Playing area**—A regulation football field is 100 yards long (the goal lines are 100 yards apart). There is an additional ten yards behind each goal line, which is called the end zone. A regulation field is 53 1/3 yards wide (see diagram this page). Organized elementary school football is played on a regulation field. However, for a choose-up game, a smaller rectangular area may be used.

2. **Football**—A regulation-size football is difficult for young boys to handle. Smaller footballs may be used.

3. **Proper equipment**—Since football is essentially a body-contact sport, proper protective equipment is necessary. Such equipment should include:
   a. Head protector or helmet
   b. Face-mask, usually attached to the headgear
   c. Mouth guard
   d. Shoulder pads
   e. Thigh pads, if the boy has football pants
   f. Gym shoes (it is not necessary that young boys wear cleated football shoes)

256

There are eleven players on a football team:

Center His job is to center the ball between his legs to the quarterback. The center also blocks.

Guards (2) They block for the ball carrier.

Tackles (2) They, too, block.

Ends (2) They block and may also catch forward passes from the quarterback and run with the ball.

Halfbacks (2) They may run with the ball, catch passes, throw passes, and block.

Fullback He, too, may run, catch passes, throw passes, and block.

Quarterback He gets the ball from the center, which starts the play. He may give the ball to another back, who will then run with it, or he may run with it himself. Or he may throw a forward pass to an end, halfback or fullback.

Players should know the following:

1. **Blocking**—Stopping an opponent by using your body. Members of the *offensive* team (team with the ball) block. When blocking, you may not grab with your hands. Your hands must remain in contact with your body. To block for a ball carrier you drive your head and shoulders into your opponent's stomach and leg area. The object is to move him out of the way so the ball carrier can get through. The lower you block, the more effective your block will be. You may also block by standing with your fists pressed against your chest, your elbows extended, and your feet wide apart. This block is used when your team is going to pass the ball.

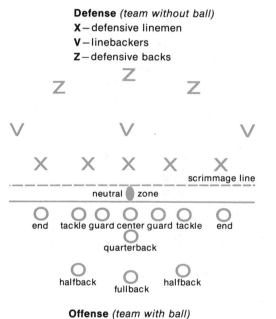

Defense *(team without ball)*
X—defensive linemen
V—linebackers
Z—defensive backs

scrimmage line
neutral zone

end tackle guard center guard tackle end
quarterback
halfback fullback halfback

Offense *(team with ball)*

2. **Tackling**—Stopping an opponent by using your body, hands, and arms. Only the *defensive* team (the team that does not have the ball) may tackle. And the defensive team may only tackle the man with the ball. The best way to tackle is from a crouched position, with your head up so you can see. You drive your shoulder into the ball carrier's legs and lock your arms around his legs to bring him to the ground. On defense you may also use your hands to avoid blockers.

3. **Kicking**

   a. *Place Kick*—A kick used to start the game (kick-off), or for extra points and field goals. On a kick-off, one team kicks the ball to the other team. One player holds the ball in an upright position on the ground with his finger. If a kicking *tee* is available, a player will not have to hold the ball. Each time a team has scored a touchdown or field goal, it kicks off to the opponent. The place kick is also used for extra points and field goals (see Scoring).

   b. *Punt*—A kick by a player on the offensive team, who drops the ball and kicks it before it touches the ground. Punting occurs when a team with the ball is giving up the ball to the opposition. The punt is used to put the ball back further from your goal line. The team that receives the punt may return it by catching it and running with it towards the goal line of the kicking team.

4. **Running**—The offensive team may run with the ball. Only the halfbacks, fullback, ends, and quarterback may run with the ball. The object is to run through the defense without being tackled and cross the goal line.

5. **Passing** — Any backfield man may throw a forward pass, but it is usually the quarterback who throws passes. A forward pass must be thrown from *behind* the line of scrimmage. Only ends, halfbacks, the fullback, or the quarterback may catch a pass. If a pass is not caught, the ball is brought back to the line of scrimmage. If the pass is intercepted by a defensive player, he may run with it. On an intercepted pass, the defensive team takes over control of the ball. A ball carrier may also throw an underhand pass, called a *lateral*, to another back or end. The lateral must be thrown to a man *behind* the ball carrier. It can never be passed to a player in front of the ball carrier. If a lateral is dropped, it is a free ball, the same as a fumble.

6. **Fumbles** — If the player with the ball drops it or has it knocked from his hands, it is a fumble. A fumble is a free ball, and the team that recovers it gains possession of the ball.

The offensive and defensive teams line up across from each other. The action is started by the offensive team. When the center snaps the ball, the play starts. The play ends when the defense tackles the ball carrier or stops a pass.

Each team has four *downs* (or plays) to move the ball. If the team with the ball gains ten yards, they are awarded a *first down*. Then they have four more downs to score or to make another first down. If the team with the ball does not score or make a first down in four downs, the ball is turned over to the opposite team.

Scoring

1. **Touchdown** — The team with the ball moves it across the goal line of the opposite team. A touchdown scores *6 points*.

2. **Extra point** — After a touchdown is made, the scoring team receives a bonus. The ball is placed two yards from the goal line. The team that has scored can either kick the ball between the goal posts and above the cross-bar and receive *1 point*; or run or pass it over the goal and receive *2 points*.

3. **Field goal** — On a regular down, a team may kick the ball through the goal posts and above the cross-bar instead of trying to make a touchdown. If the field goal is successful, it scores *3 points*.

4. **Safety** — If a player with the ball is tackled behind his own goal line, the opposite team is awarded *2 points*. The team that was caught behind its own goal must also kick off to the other team.

Penalties

When a penalty is called against a team, the opposite team can choose to accept the penalty or decline it. If the penalty is accepted, the yards are marked off by the referee and the down *does not* count. If the penalty is declined, however, the down counts. Sometimes it is better to decline a penalty, because it is more of an advantage for the team that is fouled to have the down count. *Example* — A five-yard penalty is called against the team with the ball. On the down, however, the team with the ball lost ten yards. It would be better for the defensive team to decline the penalty and have the down count, because the loss was ten yards and the penalty only five yards.

1. **Off-sides** — If either team moves across the line of scrimmage before the ball is centered, it is called off-sides. Penalty — 5 yards.

2. **Backfield in motion** — If a backfield player on the team with the ball moves forward before the ball is centered, the team is penalized 5 yards.

3. **Clipping** — If a player blocks another player from behind, it is clipping. Penalty — 15 yards.

4. **Holding** — If a player on the offensive team uses his hands in blocking or holds a defensive player, he is called for holding. Penalty — 15 yards.

5. **Unnecessary roughness** — If a player is too rough in tackling or uses more force than necessary, his team is penalized 15 yards.

6. **Pass interference** — If a player interferes with another player going for a pass before either player has actually touched the ball, his team is guilty of interference. It is not interference, however, if both players are going for the ball and accidentally bump each other. Penalty — the pass is considered complete if the foul is against the defensive team. If the foul is called against the offensive team, it is a 15-yard penalty from the line of scrimmage.

Football games have four quarters (15 minutes each). The team with the most points at the end of the game is the winner. There is no extra period if the game ends in a tie.

Touch football is played without blocking or tackling. Instead of tackling, the defensive team simply tags the ball carrier. It can be either one-hand tag or two-hand tag. This should be decided before the game starts. None of the equipment described earlier is necessary for touch football. Touch football is the type usually played in schoolyards. You can play with as few as two or three players on a team, and in an area much smaller than a regulation football field.

PROFESSIONAL SPORTS CHAMPIONS

Professional Football Champions

1982–83	Washington Redskins
1981–82	San Francisco 49ers
1980–81	Oakland Raiders
1979–80	Pittsburgh Steelers
1978–79	Pittsburgh Steelers
1977–78	Dallas Cowboys
1976–77	Oakland Raiders
1975–76	Pittsburgh Steelers
1974–75	Pittsburgh Steelers
1973–74	Miami Dolphins
1972–73	Miami Dolphins
1971–72	Dallas Cowboys
1970–71	Baltimore Colts
1969–70	Kansas City Chiefs
1968–69	New York Jets
1967–68	Green Bay Packers
1966–67	Green Bay Packers

Professional Basketball Champions

1982–83	Philadelphia 76ers
1981–82	Los Angeles Lakers
1980–81	Boston Celtics
1979–80	Los Angeles Lakers
1978–79	Seattle Super Sonics
1977–78	Washington Bullets
1976–77	Portland Trail Blazers
1975–76	Boston Celtics
1974–75	Golden State Warriors
1973–74	Boston Celtics
1972–73	New York Knicks
1971–72	Los Angeles Lakers
1970–71	Milwaukee Bucks
1969–70	New York Knicks
1968–69	Boston Celtics
1967–68	Boston Celtics
1966–67	Philadelphia 76ers
1965–66	Boston Celtics
1958–65	Boston Celtics
1957–58	St. Louis Hawks
1956–57	Boston Celtics
1955–56	Philadelphia Warriors
1954–55	Syracuse Nationals

Professional Baseball Champions

1983	Baltimore Orioles (AL)
1982	St. Louis Cardinals (NL)
1981	Los Angeles Dodgers (NL)
1980	Philadelphia Phillies (NL)
1979	Pittsburgh Pirates (NL)
1978	New York Yankees (AL)
1977	New York Yankees (AL)
1976	Cincinnati Reds (NL)
1975	Cincinnati Reds (NL)
1974	Oakland Athletics (AL)
1973	Oakland Athletics (AL)
1972	Oakland Athletics (AL)
1971	Pittsburgh Pirates (NL)
1970	Baltimore Orioles (AL)
1969	New York Mets (NL)
1968	Detroit Tigers (AL)
1967	St. Louis Cardinals (NL)
1966	Baltimore Orioles (AL)
1965	Los Angeles Dodgers (NL)
1964	St. Louis Cardinals (NL)
1963	Los Angeles Dodgers (NL)
1962	New York Yankees (AL)
1961	New York Yankees (AL)